The J(

Are you happy at work? Or do you just grin and bear it? We spend an average of 25% of our lives at work, so it's important to make the best of it.

The Joy of Work? looks at happiness and unhappiness from a fresh perspective. It draws on up-to-date research from around the world to present the causes and consequences of low job satisfaction and gives helpful suggestions and strategies for how to get more enjoyment from work. The book includes interesting case studies about individual work situations, and features simple self-completion questionnaires and procedures to help increase your happiness. Practical suggestions cover how to improve a job without moving out of it, advice about changing jobs, as well as how to alter typical styles of thinking which affect your attitudes.

This book is unique. The subject is of major significance to virtually all adults – people in jobs and those who are hoping to get one. Based on research findings, it is particularly distinctive in combining two areas that are usually looked at separately – self-help approaches to making yourself happy and issues within organizations that affect well-being.

The Joy of Work? has been written in a relaxed and readable style by an exceptional blend of authors: a highly-acclaimed professor of psychology and a widely published business journalist. Bringing together research from business and psychology – including positive psychology – this practical book will make a big difference to your happiness at work – and therefore to your whole life.

Peter Warr is Emeritus Professor at the Institute of Work Psychology at the University of Sheffield. Formerly Director of the Social and Applied Psychology Unit in that university (the world's largest research institute in its field), he has undertaken research and consultancy in hundreds of organizations.

Guy Clapperton has been a freelance business, technology and media journalist for 15 years. In 2008 he became a BAFTA juror, and is published regularly in the *Sunday Telegraph*, *Guardian*, *Times Independent* and *Financial Times*. He also broadcasts on the BBC World Service and on BBC Radio London, and has edited a number of books on employment practices.

The Joy of Work?
Jobs, Happiness, and You

Peter Warr and Guy Clapperton

Routledge
Taylor & Francis Group

LONDON AND NEW YORK

First published 2010
by Routledge
27 Church Road, Hove, East Sussex BN3 2FA

Simultaneously published in the USA and Canada
by Routledge
270 Madison Avenue, New York, NY 10016

Routledge is an imprint of the Taylor & Francis Group, an informa business

Typeset in New Century Schoolbook by Garfield Morgan,
Swansea, West Glamorgan
Printed and bound in Great Britain by TJ International Ltd
Padstow, Cornwall
Cover design by Andrew Ward

This publication has been produced with paper manufactured to strict
environmental standards and with pulp derived from sustainable forests.

British Library Cataloguing in Publication Data
A catalogue record for this book is available from the British Library

Library of Congress Cataloging in Publication Data
Warr, Peter B. (Peter Bryan)
   The joy of work? : jobs, happiness and you / Peter Warr and Guy
Clapperton.
     p. cm.
   Includes index.
   ISBN 978-0-415-45965-5 (hardcover) – ISBN 978-0-415-45966-2 (pbk.)
1. Job satisfaction. 2. Quality of work life. I. Clapperton, Guy. II. Title.
   HF5549.5.J63W367 2010
   650.1–dc22

                                                            2009011316

ISBN 978-0-415-45965-5 (hbk)
ISBN 978-0-415-45966-2 (pbk)

Contents

List of figures and questionnaires

Acknowledgments

Where did the content of this book come from? From the authors certainly, but also from a lot of other people. We've talked with many individuals about jobs and their feelings and have read a large number of articles and books. The ideas which follow have many sources, and we are widely grateful.

We particularly thank the interviewees quoted throughout the chapters, those who offered interviews for which space was unavailable, and the publisher's reviewers of an initial draft who made many valuable suggestions. So too did colleagues current and over the years, although most of those could not have known of this book at the time. Thank you all very much.

Work and happiness: An unlikely mix?

Some jobs are awful through and through, and some are simply great. But most are in-between – a mixture of the good and the bad. Working[1]* involves doing things you don't want to do as well as (in most cases) doing what you enjoy. So it's not surprising that people view it in contrasting ways.

You can see the two different outlooks in society across the ages. The Bible, in the Book of Genesis, saw it as punishment for original sin: only "in the sweat of thy face shalt thou eat bread." Medieval work almost always involved hard physical slog and all the potential for pain and damage that involved, and later on Adam Smith (1723–1790) argued that repetitive work made people "as stupid and ignorant as it is possible for a human being to become."

Joking about the nastiness of work, Alfred Polgar (1873–1955) suggested it's "what you do so that some time you won't have to do it any more." Nowadays, articles in newspapers and magazines (not to mention all those blogs) focus on the horrors of a job rather than exploring its benefits, and television plays and "soaps" rely on the workplace and other workers to create obstacles to a story's successful outcome.

And then there's the impact of Dennis the Menace and others of his kind. Dennis is the cover character of Britain's

---

* Throughout the book, reference Notes are listed at the end of a chapter.

best-selling children's weekly, the *Beano*, and also a successful cartoon character with a popular namesake in the USA. He has his own annual book and has held the *Beano* cover position for more than three decades appearing every week since 1951. Generations of young people have empathized with his activities. Dennis's view of work is clear – it's bad!

He is basically a workshy child, who'd prefer to be out fighting against authority rather than doing anything constructive, although the American version tends more to cuteness than anarchy. The UK version has an enemy called Walter who suffers terribly at Dennis's hands. Walter is a Softy, partly because he likes school. Instead, Dennis makes it clear that he hates work of any kind. He's great fun, but is also a role model telling us early in life that work and discipline are bad.

This anti-work outlook is not restricted to Dennis the Menace, of course. For example, there's also been Bart Simpson: avoiding school, with no real aptitude for work, and worshipping his equally idle father, Homer. Neither will willingly put in an honest day's toil, and that's why they're "cool." The Simpsons have huge numbers of followers all over the globe. *Just William, Horrid Henry, Minnie the Minx* and other popular books and comic strips are full of these downbeats – they're massively popular and they're massively anti-work. All of them convey a powerful message early in life.

There are also more mature examples. The British poet Philip Larkin (1922–1985) asked in the first line of his poem *Toads*:

Why should I let the toad *work*
Squat on my life?

Got the picture? A generally negative image of work is emphasized around us. From childhood to adult years we are encouraged to see it as bad.

However, another view has also long been argued. Martin Luther (1436–1546) claimed that "the human being is created to work as the bird is created to fly," and John

Calvin (1509–1564) thought work for its own sake would offer its own rewards. His views were particularly important in forming the Protestant work ethic, which was based on both religious and worldly benefits – hard work is good because it helps you to get to Heaven as well as perhaps making you wealthy. Look also at George Berkeley (1658–1753), who considered "there can be no such thing as a happy life without labour," or Thomas Hobbes (1588–1679) who said "work is good; it truly is a motive for life." Thomas Carlyle (1795–1881) was another great fan: "there is a perennial nobleness, and even sacredness, in work."

Early Puritans emphasized a different kind of value; work prevented idleness which exposed people to all sorts of opportunities for sin. Samuel Pepys (1633–1703) gave us another theme; he liked to stay late in his office because that meant he didn't have to go home to quarrel with his wife.

Sigmund Freud (1856–1939) didn't only talk about love and sex; he saw work as one of the main pillars of a healthy life. Noel Coward (1899–1973) even suggested that work was "much more fun than fun." You probably think that Henry Ford (1863–1947) went over the top when he claimed that "work is our sanity, our self-respect, our salvation. So far from being a curse, work is the greatest blessing." Nevertheless, recent surveys have shown that the majority of workers – 70% plus – say they're satisfied with what they do. And let's not forget that Philip Larkin wrote a sequel to the poem we quoted earlier – *Toads Revisited* – in which he acknowledged that in middle age he rather liked the old toad of work.

You probably don't often stop to think about it, but work is widely valued as a central part of life.

You're born, and before too long you have to start spending most of your time working to sustain yourself. Along with love and your physical being, work is key to your existential circumstances. Who am I? What do I want? What is my place in the world and my status in it? Am I useful? Am I fulfilled? . . . Work defines, to a large degree, your external identity as part of the social matrix.

But it also looms very large in your inner sense of how you're traveling through life.[2]

So work is both a bad thing and a good thing. However, as children and adults we have been encouraged by popular culture to emphasize the negative and to play down the idea that jobs can contribute to our happiness.

This book recognizes the harm that jobs can cause – the tiredness, anxiety, back pain, reduced family time, and so on – but builds on the positive potential that exists in nearly every one. Most of us can't avoid working – it takes up around a third of our life – so let's enjoy it as much as we can. Writing in *The Times* on 10 January 2009, Janice Turner was troubled by the anti-job prejudice she saw among young girls. Her message was clear: "Work is good, it can even be noble. It can make us forget ourselves. That is what we should tell our daughters. It can be hard, thankless, scary, joyless at times. But you will feel useful, purposeful, part of the world."

In these pages we'll look into the principal features of jobs, and explore the way those might be changed. The chapters will be based on research by psychologists from all over the world, shedding light on issues facing all of us but rarely escaping from the pages of academic journals. We'll also talk to people – quote actual examples of what they have done about their jobs. However, the book doesn't only identify the causes of happiness or unhappiness in jobs; we'll set out some courses of action. There are inevitably limits, but it's usually possible to do something to increase your work happiness. It's certainly worth looking at the possibilities.

Key concepts

Let's run through some of the notions we'll be dealing with. "Work" is in general a question of doing something you "have to" do, and it's likely to require exertion and be arduous, burdensome, or "hard work" for at least part of the time. In this book we're usually referring to paid work. For most people that involves being a full-time employee of someone else, but it can be self-employment or part-time employment. And you can also "work" in other ways which don't involve payment, such as housework, voluntary work and do-it-yourself work; many of the book's themes also apply there, although those activities are not the primary concern here.

The other notion we'll be discussing is "happiness." Most of us recognize this when we feel it, but finding a precise definition is like nailing down soot. For centuries, philosophers have struggled to analyze what it means, and general agreement has proven all but impossible. For now, let's just say that it's a state of feeling good, and that unhappiness is feeling bad. That will be made more definite in Chapter 3. Our terms will be mostly psychological, but we'll be relating those to people's day-to-day experience. We'll identify different kinds of happiness and unhappiness, as well as their likely causes.

The word's root comes from Middle English – "hap" which means chance or luck. Think about "happenstance" and "haplessness" and you'll see we still have the original meaning buried in other words. The modern definition owes less to luck than to the deliberate efforts of the happy individual, and a lot of it comes from factors within the person rather than merely from outside.

By the end of the book you should be clear why some people are happier or unhappier at work than others. For a start, job title might provide a clue. Several studies indicate that people in certain kinds of job are in general happier or less happy than others. In one British investigation, gardeners, hairdressers and care assistants were among the most satisfied, while bus drivers, postal workers and assembly line workers were among the least. Another study found that the happiest workers included chefs and members of the clergy, while architects and secretaries were the least happy in their jobs. Research in the USA has revealed that managers and administrators are among the most satisfied, whereas the lowest-scorers include machine operators and laborers.

These sorts of study are a start, but a job title on its own doesn't tell us much by way of explanation. There has to be more to it than that, particularly since people with the same title can have different experiences. For example, job satisfaction depends partly on your age (it's lowest on average between 35 and 45). And the content of two jobs with the same title can vary considerably, depending for instance on the size of the company and the nature of the business. Even if we could be certain that job title alone had some sort of connection with people's happiness at work, it wouldn't be all that useful as information about the sources of their good or bad feelings.

To make sense of job title patterns, you have to look deeper. What is it about different job titles and the activities that go with them which makes people happy or unhappy? It's here that the research becomes particularly interesting and applicable to all of us. If you can identify the components that go into a job to make someone happy, then perhaps you can fit some into your own job. Or perhaps you might be able to reflect on your position in those terms and reassess your state of mind while you're at work.

Levels of short-term happiness and long-term happiness can coincide, but they don't always. Happiness can be associated with a single event but it's also a continuing state of mind. During the course of the book we'll be considering these various forms of happiness, looking at what stimulates them, and suggesting how they might perhaps be increased. And of course we'll also be covering the bad feelings – unhappiness in its several forms.

Why does it matter?

There are many reasons for taking these issues seriously, whether you're an employer wanting a more fulfilled and productive workforce or an employee wishing for a more fulfilling life. Quite simply, happiness is a principal objective in life. People will always seek it, for themselves and for their family, friends, colleagues, staff and others. That is enough of a reason to write books about it.

Indeed, there have been many such books. They range from academic volumes by philosophers, historians and psychologists (even by economists in recent years) to suggestions about how to reduce your own distress. Happiness and unhappiness are popular topics for television programs and magazine articles, usually dealing with a particular lifestyle issue likely to interest their audience or readership. Themes might cover "How married people can stay happy," "Be happy during the credit crunch," or "Eat your way to happiness."

But where do you find books and articles about being happy in your job? Those are few and far between, even though almost everyone spends a large proportion of their time at work. No one doubts that happiness is important and deserves discussion in nonwork situations, but popular media often give the impression that happiness issues disappear once you set foot in the workplace. That is nonsense. People want to be happy in their jobs, just as elsewhere, and many are not happy there. Many of the same issues deserve attention in both work and nonwork settings.

Another way in which happiness is an important topic comes from the effect it has on behavior and social relationships. Let's start in the workplace. Happy people will generally contribute more to an organization than their less happy counterparts. Research investigations by psychologists in many countries have revealed a general association between positive job feelings and performance in a job. More satisfied employees are likely to achieve more work goals. They will also be absent less often and remain with their organization for a longer time; if you don't enjoy your job, you're probably interested in finding another one. (And, to be mercenary for a moment, the cost to an employer of replacing a good worker can run into thousands of pounds or dollars; losing a lot of good workers because they're unhappy costs a lot of thousands.)

There's more. Satisfied workers have been shown to be more cooperative and supportive of colleagues, to provide stronger support to others in difficult times, and to be generally more willing to "go the extra mile" for their colleagues. Psychologists refer to that as "organizational citizenship behavior" and the evidence is clear: less satisfied employees are less good citizens in their organization. Happier employees also contribute to their greater job success by showing more initiative – looking out for problems in advance and finding their own solutions, rather than merely sitting back and waiting for someone else to sort things out. More extremely, a happy employee is also less likely to steal company property, introduce viruses on a memory stick, or – as in the legendary story of the disgruntled woman on being sacked – phone the speaking clock in another country and leave the line open all weekend.

These patterns don't just involve individuals on their own. Cheerful behavior also encourages positive reactions from other people. The colleagues of a happy worker have been found to respond more positively to him or her. People in a positive mood are treated by others in a more friendly way and helped more, so that together a positive group morale is built up. This is the notion of "reciprocity," a central theme in social psychological thinking – we tend to give back what we receive. Overall, happy people's better social relationships were described in a recent review of research as "one of the most robust findings in the literature."

Of course, these are broad conclusions and not uniformities. Unhappy workers do not all behave in exactly the same way, and some are undoubtedly good at their jobs. But the fact remains that extensive research has demonstrated general links between being happier in your job and being better at that job. We want to emphasize that we are not simply stating our own opinions – there are a lot of those around in books about happiness – we have reviewed in detail a large number of research publications.

There have also been studies that look at organizations as a whole – showing that companies with higher average employee happiness also have better financial performance and customer satisfaction. The well-being of staff can have a material effect on a company's bottom-line profits, and nobody should think otherwise. That has to be the classic win–win situation.

The reverse sequence also occurs. Good performance at work can itself promote well-being, as effective work leads to satisfaction with what you have achieved, new personal opportunities, appreciation from customers, and possibly an increased salary. More generally, research has consistently shown that success breeds happiness as well as happiness leading to success.

There are a lot of factors associated with these issues, as we'll examine later. There are also apparent contradictions, for example the idea that if you want people to be happy at work then it's good to let them manage themselves, but they still need to be supervised. Sometimes it's important to look for the "happy medium," rather than seek the maximum amount of a possible feature.

And there's no escaping the fact that even happy people have periods of unhappiness. Indeed, there is a sense in which you often can't have one without the other. That's the "no pain, no gain" idea which can keep sportspeople battling on (through the "pain barrier") and overweight dieters struggling for a little bit longer. It's certainly not always the case, but happiness does often depend on achieving goals which have required you to struggle for a period, probably feeling anxious, worried and generally anything but happy. You will undoubtedly experience tension and distress on your way to some kinds of happiness – that's life.

In this book

As a sort of road-map for where we're going, here's an outline of the later chapters.

Chapter 2 looks at motivation – why do people want a job? Take a colleague of ours who is freelance and has erratic income. Why, you might ask, would any sane person opt for such an unsteady life with so little chance of budgeting sensibly or organizing regular working hours? He has answers, making the point that there's a lot more to work motivation than the purely financial.

The next chapter covers happiness itself – joy, exuberance, comfort and calmness – balanced against the unhappy downside – anxiety, depression and similar feelings. We'll provide questionnaires for you to do a bit of self-testing, and also look at the popular notion of "job satisfaction." This chapter will give you an idea of the different kinds of happiness or unhappiness that may be important for you.

In the fourth chapter we move to look at everyday features that are fundamental to feeling good or bad. We'll do that in terms of the "Needed Nine" key elements in any situation – in your family, leisure activities, or wherever. These include features such as having some influence over what happens to you, a moderate level of demands, good social contacts, and a role that you value – and not forgetting money. Chapter 4 will look also at people who are unemployed or retired and those who are caring for their family perhaps in between paid jobs. How do these people's lives stack up in terms of the Needed Nine features?

Chapters 5 and 6 transfer the Needed Nine aspects of life into the workplace, looking at how these sources of good or bad feelings operate in a job. We'll see that for jobs it's essential to add three more features – having supportive bosses, a good career outlook, and organizational fairness. Altogether, we thus examine what are labeled as the "Top Twelve" features in any job – the ones that really matter for happiness or unhappiness. Focusing on your own position, another questionnaire is provided for you to create a profile of your own job in those terms.

The next two chapters look at happiness influences within you rather than in your situation. There's no doubt the same job can be experienced differently by different people, and that's partly a question of their genes – what they were born with. Research evidence is mounting that people carry round their own "baseline" of low or high happiness, and that this is largely inherited. Chapter 7 will review that evidence, and show that happiness and unhappiness are linked to certain traits of continuing personality.

In Chapter 8 we'll put these elements against different personal preferences, work values, and ways of thinking about jobs. Writing about 400 years ago, William Shakespeare made one of his characters point out (in disagreement with others about how to view a situation) that "there is nothing either good or bad, but thinking makes it so."[3]

That's something of an overstatement, since a minority of situations are undoubtedly good or bad in themselves, but the point is widely valid: happiness can very much depend on how you view things.

For instance, we mustn't forget different kinds of "social comparisons," when people's happiness depends on their view of what other people are getting (yes, "keeping up with the Joneses" comes in here). And processes of adaptation need to be looked at: how far do people become used to whatever conditions they are in? There are plenty of examples around of workers who are less happy or less unhappy than an observer might expect. Looking also at individual preferences we'll provide another questionnaire, for you to profile what it is that matters to you in a job.

The final two chapters turn the book's key themes into possible action – asking what you can do to make yourself happier at work, given that completely throwing in a job of any kind is not a realistic option. There won't be any quick fixes because there aren't any, but we hope that the suggested steps in Chapters 9 and 10 will help you to emerge more happy than when you started the book. We'll review your current situation, and also look at nonjob features like your personality and typical ways of thinking, and then ask about possible ways to improve things. As throughout the book, we'll be writing for you personally and also for managers who might want to consider what could be useful in their organization.

So here's a brief aside for managers. You are undoubtedly interested in your own happiness, but you may forget how much your day-to-day decisions affect the happiness or unhappiness of your staff. That matters to them, and it should matter to you for the very practical, bottom-line reasons outlined earlier. Of course, effectiveness and financial results must generally be your top priority, and we know that some workers will probably have to be unhappy about some aspects of their work if the company is to succeed. Nevertheless, Chapter 10 sets out straightforward steps managers can take to balance the two goals – employee well-being and organizational success. It's important not to think only in terms of the second of those.

A general point here concerns the notion of "morale." If you feel that your staff's "happiness" or "well-being" sounds a bit too wishy-washy, think and talk instead about morale. Everyone wants increased morale, and we'll show in Chapter 3 that this is a principal form of happiness in work settings.

Finally at this point you should heed a few words of warning about what this book doesn't set out to do. It doesn't provide a way of coping with clinical depression or other genuine mental ill-health issues. Nor does it offer overnight solutions: happiness often takes time. And not all parts of the book will apply to everyone. For example, there's no point in looking for a higher-paid job if you're already earning a fortune, or seeking more challenge if you're already overwhelmed. Nevertheless, we do believe that research findings applied in a practical manner can make a substantial difference. We'd be surprised if every reader did not find something here that could be helpful.

Of course, there are a lot of books out there that deal with happiness, how to lift yourself out of a trough, or why you're down there in the first place. This is certainly in that ball-park, but it sets out to be different.

Note first that most of the other books around don't mention jobs and paid work – they are dealing with personal and relationship problems for which they treat jobs as irrelevant. Second, what we'll be saying has its origins in an extensive body of research findings by academic psychologists across the world. We're able to draw on a firm evidence base, both from a comprehensive review of those findings by Professor Peter Warr[4] and from psychologists' research published even more recently. (A Further Reading section is included at the end of the book.) The addition of real-life examples from Guy Clapperton's journalistic experience adds a grounding that a purely academic work lacks. The book is thus very different from reportage-led pieces without the knowledge of psychology through which many of the motivations and outcomes in this book have been illuminated. It is both scientifically authoritative and, we hope, pleasant to read.

In 1937, American brothers George and Ira Gershwin wrote a very successful song called "Nice Work If You Can Get It." They were writing about the happiness of a "girl and boy" rather than in a job, but their main theme (for nice work you've got to try) applies in our area too. Although we can't all get "nice work" of the paid kind, most of us can find work that is "nicer" – but only "if you try."

Notes

1 Our focus here is on jobs, and when we refer simply to "work" or "working" we're usually talking about a job. However, there are many other kinds of "work" – housework, voluntary work, do-it-yourself work, and so on. Activities can be similar in all kinds, but the big difference is that in a job you get paid.

2 See the Introduction to J. Bowe, M. Bowe, and S. Streeter (eds.) *Gig: Americans talk about their jobs* (New York: Three Rivers Press, 2000).

3 From *Hamlet* Act 2 Scene 2 when talking about his country: is that like a prison to its inhabitants?

4 *Work, happiness, and unhappiness*, published by Routledge (New York) in 2007. That book contains more than a thousand research references supporting chapters in the present volume.

Why work?

Loads of people love their jobs and hate them too. There are many reasons for mixed feelings like that and we'll be looking at those throughout the book, but there's no getting away from the fact that jobs sometimes make us do things we don't want to do – either at any time at all, or just at this particular moment when the television, pub, child's school play, shopping mall or whatever is more attractive. People are stuck with activities they don't like but which have to be done.

In that sense jobs can clearly be a "bad thing." As Chapter 1 showed, though, they're also a "good thing" in other ways, and there's a lot of evidence that most adults want to have a job. They won't be happy all the time when they're working in that job, but they do want to work somewhere. That's because they need the money, sure, but also for several other reasons. There can be many satisfactions and pleasures, and we'll look at these shortly.

There's also the fact that it's the norm; people expect you to have a job; it's a given if you're within working age. A colleague was at college during the last height of unemployment in the 1980s when over 3 million people out of a UK working population of 30 million or so were without a job. He lodged in the same house as someone who didn't have a job, and, although his status as a student was no more "employed" than that of his fellow lodger, it was the other person who was made to feel uncomfortable about his lack of occupation; the student had a "proper" role in society.

This chapter will look at our love–hate relationship with paid work. First, we'll review some ways in which having a job matters to people, and then we'll see how joblessness can have its effects. We'll look at research into unemployment – when a lack of work is involuntary – and retirement, which is clearly more voluntary. Studies of subjective well-being in those two conditions will point us to the main reasons for wanting a job – and thus to many of the sources of happiness or unhappiness in work.

What's the point of having a job?

Newspapers love stories about lottery winners choosing to continue working despite being rich, and there are many such people (although they may look for a different kind of job, or one that isn't full-time). Countless surveys have asked people whether they would continue working after a lottery win or a big inheritance,[1] and more than half the population say they expect to stay in a job if they become wealthy. Of course, few people know precisely how they'd behave under those circumstances, so replies can be a bit uncertain, but the usual intention is clearly to keep up a paid occupation.

People also work at a job in an unpaid capacity. One of the book's authors, Peter Warr, is an "emeritus professor" at the University of Sheffield, which means that he doesn't get paid for working there. He remains happy carrying out research and writing articles and books because there are other motivations, such as gaining new ideas and social contacts, achieving targets, contributing to others, and keeping involved in a wide range of activities. Contrast this with the famous quote variously attributed to Boswell or Johnson that "No one but a blockhead ever wrote except for money" – whichever one said that was simply wrong.

Work motivations can change over different periods in someone's life. The book's other author, Guy Clapperton, secured his first after-college job in a local charity, working from someone's home office. He found after a year or so that the environment was wrong for him, and he wasn't meeting any people his own age (and, yes, for "people" you can probably read "young women" – hey, I was only just out of college, I was single . . .). The work itself, although not very hands-on, was satisfying, the journey to work undemanding, and the much older people he did meet were perfectly pleasant. He also found the idea of having a title ("coordinator") appealed to what he had yet to identify as insecurity due to professional inexperience.

Nevertheless, when he made the switch to a central London magazine office with a daily hour-long commute but with lively individuals sharing a similar outlook and in many cases inexperience of life, his happiness went up considerably even though there was a pay cut. At that stage in his life the social elements of work and the longer-term prospects were particularly important.

Your attitude to having a job can also change as you become more settled in it. One of the people we talked with when writing this book was Pamela Goldberg, the chief executive of the Breast Cancer Campaign. "I really thought when I got married that was it, I'd be a wife and a mother and that sort of thing," she says. Without huge enthusiasm, she took a job as a personal assistant when her husband started some study, and discovered that she really liked working. "I've worked ever since and done a lot of different things, but when I became involved in the charity and subsequently started running it, I realized I was very happy." The "running it" bit is important to Pamela Goldberg, although it wouldn't be to everyone, because it aligns her work to her personality.

Jobs give you opportunities to do something that you couldn't otherwise do – become a computer expert, drive a huge lorry, acquire unusual skills, meet interesting people, coordinate large projects, design buildings or dresses, teach young people, or even travel to exciting places. There's another aspect to that. The demands created by a job can draw you out of yourself and reduce the worries that can grow if you're sitting around doing nothing.

Eddie Nestor is a name well-known to London-based readers. At the time of writing he presents the *Drivetime* show on BBC Radio London. He used to have a Sunday morning show but this was moved to late Sunday night, without his complete enthusiasm. The Sunday morning show was exceptionally good, receiving a Sony radio award (Sony being the UK radio equivalent of an Oscar or Bafta). The award was made three days after he had a dose of chemotherapy for Hodgkins' Lymphoma, and unsurprisingly he was feeling rough. "I've got to go and win it again now, so I can enjoy it," he quips. "I couldn't taste any of the food at the ceremony. I shouldn't really have been there but you can't miss that night, can you?"

The task ahead of Nestor was clearly to keep himself motivated through his period of illness. He did this, he says, through a number of means. First the BBC allowed him to web-log or blog the entire experience. "The things I looked forward to were writing the blog and Thursdays. All Thursdays were good. I had treatment on a Friday and came back to work on Thursday [to do his other regular show], so I looked forward to that." Getting to work was important to Eddie, extending his horizons, giving him targets, and pushing him to keep at things. As this book went to press he has been in remission for some time and continues working successfully on the same radio station.

Sigmund Freud and his fellow psychoanalysts have a lot to answer for, but they had some intriguing ideas about the importance of work. Freud described it as people's strongest tie to their world, valuably preventing them from being overwhelmed by their own feelings. His colleagues developed this idea to talk about "Sunday neuroses." At a time when Sunday was the only day without work (OK, housework wasn't considered for predominantly male clients), people became more unhappy – their neurotic and psychosomatic symptoms increased in comparison to working days. That was attributed to the fact that, in the absence of job pressures, people can become more troubled by personal issues which they can otherwise put on one side during a busy week.

The idea was extended also to holidays beyond merely Sundays, and there's certainly something in it: some individuals are unsettled by the lack of demands on them when they're not doing their job. They become uneasy and their anxiety spreads into other activities. That's another reason to view work as a "good thing" for them personally, although we do wonder where it sometimes leaves members of their family.

A sense of personal emptiness linked to doing nothing can be strong during unemployment, and it's sometimes a problem when people retire. As we'll review later, many of the more successfully retired people are those who find themselves one or more alternative roles – either paid or unpaid. A 66-year-old retired school principal now works part-time as a "greeter," welcoming customers as they arrive at a supermarket. He describes other retired colleagues who "like to get out of the house, to have something to do . . . Nowadays people want to get out and do more. And people are healthier and live longer too . . . I've got years to go before I want to quit working here. I like it and it keeps me busy."[2]

But what about the money? We're told that money makes the world go round. You wouldn't commit yourself to commute long distances at unpleasant times and to do many of the dreary things you're asked to do in a job unless you got paid. Indeed, for some people a job is wanted and tolerated almost entirely because it's the only way to get essential money. For others, once pay is roughly enough, attention switches to other possible benefits. Those people are certainly looking for an income that is broadly OK, but beyond that it's other features that count. A good job's attraction is a lot more than money. Paid work provides psychologically important features which turn out to be among the principal sources of happiness anywhere. Take those features away, as in unemployment or in other settings, and unhappiness will usually follow.

So what are the benefits from working? If we could identify them in general terms, we could analyze the content of any job: how far does it have the psychologically important features? There's been a lot of research into the qualities of good and bad jobs (and we'll get there soon), but researchers have also learned a lot from a different kind of investigation – examining nonworkers, in particular those who are unemployed.

Unemployment: What's missing?

It seems strange now, but some politicians and others in the 1970s were reluctant to believe that forced unemployment was psychologically harmful. Joblessness was increasing rapidly in that decade, and politicians didn't want to be blamed for their constituents' psychological ill-health. There was also a reluctance in some quarters to admit that unemployment was anything other than idleness. It became clear, just as it had done in the 1930s, that this belief was wide of the mark, and it's now firmly established that failing to get a job can make people feel very distressed indeed. (And attitudes to mental health have changed a lot since those earlier years.) These three unemployed individuals know what it's like:

> You feel as though your whole life is crumbling. You feel devalued out of work; you feel your age, you feel you have less and less to offer. Instead of feeling you're getting richer in experience, you feel something is being taken away from you . . . You lead a sort of double life: the pointlessness of the daily round, and the knowledge that you are still a feeling, thinking human being whose skills and talents are lying unused.

> It's bad and has to be respected as much as someone who's lost a leg . . . . I lived in a mental shell, not talking about what the real problems are . . . I was totally crushed by the whole thing.

> You don't realize what [work] means to you. I worked with three good blokes over ten years. You get to know them, you respect them, you know all about their families . . . But if I see them now, there's none of them working, we haven't anything to say to each other.[3]

However, unemployment isn't just for men; it's a women's issue too. Especially as women increasingly view paid work as an important part of their life, losing a job can be traumatic. Until 1990, East Germany was a communist country in which women and men were treated equally in employment roles. After East and West Germany were unified, unemployment soared in the east. Many women in particular found themselves near to despair as they had hitherto largely defined themselves by their jobs. Here are some reactions.[4]

> I fell into a really deep hole. I delivered newspapers and my husband sold insurance. I constantly had tears in my eyes. We just couldn't face not working.

> It's not only the financial side but there is also a considerable psychological burden as we are just not used to not working. I'm a career woman and I cannot come to terms with this rut that I'm stuck in. It's just impossible to bear.

> I've got no role any more . . . I want a job as I am something then but now I am nothing.

The pains of unemployment have been detailed by research investigations of several kinds. Most straightforward are comparisons between employed and unemployed samples, where sure enough people without a job show substantially more distress and unhappiness. But perhaps the distressed unemployed people have always been like that? That's an unlikely explanation, but some 1970s politicians did suggest it. Studies which track the same individuals from a job to unemployment or in the reverse direction would surely settle it. And they do: people's mental health gets worse in lots of ways when they lose a job, and it improves when they get back to work. That has been found in many countries and also in better economic conditions than the 1970s. In fact, studies have shown how losing a job in good financial times can be particularly troublesome; when everyone else seems to have a job, the stigma of unemployment can be even worse.

What are these psychological effects of not having a job when you want one? Psychologists have used questionnaires and interviews to look at different aspects of distress, low self-esteem, low self-confidence, anxiety, depression, life dissatisfaction, and general unhappiness. (We'll look more at these aspects of unhappiness in Chapter 3.) Across a wide range of unhappiness indicators, the harmful impact of becoming unemployed is repeatedly found to be substantial, as are the improvements when people get back into a job.

And distress is not only an individual matter: the negative impact can spread through a person's family, harming the way he or she gets on with other people and helps them to deal with their own problems. Many studies have shown how depression, anxiety and a loss of self-confidence can flow across into relations with children and a partner, creating frequent squabbles about activities and the family's shortage of money. One man reported:

> I think the family started deteriorating [after about a month] . . . I was easily angry and upset, and I used to snap at the children all the time . . . I would do nothing constructive around the house – just sit around with no energy, I didn't want to go out of the doorstep. Nobody could talk to me and I had nothing to talk about.[5]

Part of the change in people when they lose their job is a general slowing down and the gradual development of a sense that you can't be bothered to exert yourself. Sociologist Paul Lazarsfeld described in an Austrian community "the vicious cycle between reduced opportunities and reduced level of aspiration" in which "prolonged unemployment leads to a state of apathy in which the victims do not utilize any longer even the few opportunities left to them." That was in the 1930s when material conditions were worse than nowadays, but experiences of that kind are still common; it's very hard to press yourself to make big efforts and take initiatives when you've been out of work for a long period.

Why should enforced joblessness have those effects? What's missing from an unemployed person's life? An obvious answer (again!) is "money." Most unemployed people are substantially poorer than they were when in a job; in some cases they're really struggling financially to make ends meet. It's not surprising that studies have repeatedly found raised levels of financial anxiety and distress among those who have lost their jobs. Less dramatic but still a big shock for some who are made redundant is the sudden loss of perks – free telephone calls, stationery, or even a company car.

But some people (often managers) are given a monetary "cushion" when they become unemployed, and a few others can manage financially even without a job. Why should becoming unemployed make those people unhappy? This question was answered for unemployed people generally by social psychologist Marie Jahoda around 1980 in terms of five "latent functions" of a job – personal benefits which are more hidden than is work's "manifest function" of earning money. Let's look at those.

First, being employed creates a structure to your day, splitting it into chunks: you have to start on time, fit within schedules, and generally organize yourself to meet external requirements. Without those must-do activities, many people lose their sense of time and come to find themselves in an unchanging world, with nothing to break up the day, doing the same activities, in a fixed setting, with no novelty, and having no interests outside their little setting.

Second, having a job makes you part of a larger social network, reduces isolation and loneliness, and gives you shared experiences with others. In your work you meet new and perhaps interesting people. There are also the ones you don't like, but the general point is that people need contact with others and without a job those contacts can be severely reduced.

Marie Jahoda's third "latent function" was described in terms of goals and purposes that go beyond your own. Being drawn out of yourself is important for its own sake, introducing you to challenges and other people's needs, but also because the routines of work become comforting in their familiarity. It's often a nice feeling to be settled in activities that are a regular part of your life.

Fourth, employment helps to provide a sense of identity, a view of yourself and how you fit into the wider scheme of things. As part of that, being without a job can bring terrible stigma, at least as seen by the person involved. He or she can feel like a failure, "on the scrap-heap," not playing a proper part in society or in support of one's family. Finally, having a job enforces activity, provides objectives and purposes, and makes you keep going rather than turning in on yourself and perhaps ruminating about your problems (back to "Sunday neuroses" again).

During the 1980s and 1990s psychologists carried out many studies comparing the activities of employed and unemployed individuals, and sure enough there were substantial differences in those aspects of their life – they were effectively in different worlds. Unemployed people are not only short of money, they also have limited time structure, social contacts, external goals, social status, and levels of activity – the five "latent functions" of a job.

Of course, there are also differences between the situations of people all of whom are unemployed. Researchers have also looked at those – comparing between different jobless people, rather than only contrasting unemployment in general against having a job in general. Distress levels in different unemployed individuals turn out to be linked directly to lower levels of these job "functions" in their world: the more an unemployed person lacks the features in his or her own setting, the more unhappy he or she is. We'll include and develop the ideas of Marie Jahoda in later chapters, showing there how you can profile your own situation or job in terms like those.

This chapter's focus on unemployment has pointed to key differences between enforced joblessness and the situation of people in jobs. However, features that make the difference between those two groups are also found elsewhere – for instance in the lives of retired people and of "home-makers." Can't we explain their happiness or unhappiness in the same terms? Yes we can. Chapter 4 will show how that can be done, after the findings outlined here have been combined with later research results.

First, however, we need a clearer idea about "happiness" and "unhappiness." Those are the topics of Chapter 3.

Notes

1 As is the case throughout the book, detailed references to cited research are provided in the academic volume associated with this one: *Work, happiness, and unhappiness*, by Peter Warr, published by Routledge, New York in 2007.

2 See page 4 of J. Bowe, M. Bowe, and S. Streeter (eds.) *Gig: Americans talk about their jobs* (New York: Three Rivers Press, 2000).

3 These quotations are referenced on page 59 of *Work, unemployment and mental health* by Peter Warr (Oxford: Oxford University Press, 1987).

4 These quotations are from "Resilience and unemployment: A case study of East German women", written by Vanessa Beck, Debbie Wagener and Jonathan Grix, and published in *German Politics*, 2005, 14, 1–13.

5 From page 170 of *The forsaken families* by Leonard Fagin and Martin Little (Harmondsworth: Penguin, 1984).

Feeling good and feeling bad

Are you happy at work? Many people, on hearing that sort of question, go a bit shruggy. They don't really know, they'll tell you; what's happy, after all they do the job, it pays the bills, what else is there? Others say they sometimes quite like their job but often they don't, so they're not really sure. Or maybe they feel OK about it, but does that make them happy? Finding a definition is tricky. In this chapter we'll look at some of the main approaches taken in academic research to see how they can help us.

Test yourself – can't get no satisfaction?

Let's begin by looking at your own feelings. To find out how happy or unhappy you are, we need a bit more than gut feeling.

Our starting point is the idea of work satisfaction. People sometimes say "my job satisfaction is low" or "that episode really affected my job satisfaction," and satisfaction or dissatisfaction are certainly forms of happiness or unhappiness respectively. Many surveys have shown that between about 70% and 90% of people are satisfied with their jobs, but the actual percentage differs according to where the cut-off is set for being "really" satisfied.

Your feelings of job satisfaction are in part based on what you can expect in the circumstances. If no other suitable jobs are available, you may decide you're satisfied with what you've got, even though you don't much like it. In that case you could be using "satisfactory" rather like a school teacher would on an old-fashioned school report, where it would sometimes mean a bit "nondescript." So people's levels of reported job satisfaction may be higher than their happiness levels measured in other ways – the job will do, but it's not great and doesn't really make them "happy."

That said, job satisfaction questionnaires are a good but partial way to learn about workers' feelings. Measurement questionnaires are of two kinds. The first asks global questions about a job overall. For example, one rather direct overall question asks how much you agree with "All things considered, I'm satisfied with my job." The second approach covers separate satisfactions with principal aspects – pay, working conditions, hours of work, colleagues, and so on, and provides more detailed information. The different facet satisfactions can be combined into an overall score, or particular groups of items can indicate people's satisfaction with a subset of job features.

Questionnaire 1 (pages 30–31) is a job satisfaction questionnaire that has been applied around the world.[1] Try filling it in. No, don't hum and hah and just read on, really fill it in. It might be a good idea to photocopy the pages or simply write down the numbers of your answers, because you could do the questionnaire again later if things change or if you move to a different job. Also give photocopies to friends and colleagues – it's a way of finding out how your view stacks up against theirs. Or you could print out a copy from www.psypress.com/joyofwork. Don't forget to record the date, so that you can compare today against any later answers you may give.

You'll see that this questionnaire looks at overall job satisfaction by considering 15 main features. You obtain an overall score by adding together your 15 responses and then dividing by 15 to give an average answer.

If you're typical of the UK population, your average score across all the items on Questionnaire 1 is likely to be between four and five. In a sample of nearly 50,000 UK workers the average response was found to be 4.47,[2] with women scoring on average just slightly more than men. But of course you may have different feelings about different aspects of your job. It's useful to look at, say, the three items on which you scored highest and lowest. Is that pattern acceptable to you? Can you do anything to change it? We'll look at possible answers to those questions in Chapters 9 and 10.

Understanding your personal mix

Everyone has a mass of feelings which overlap with each other. For a start, let's divide feelings into three different levels of scope: global, domain-specific and facet-specific. At the first level, "global happiness" or "global unhappiness" is your overall feeling about life – "I'm generally happy about things," "Life could be a lot better," and other all-things-considered reactions. "Life satisfaction" is one aspect of this global feeling. Second, "domain-specific happiness" concerns particular parts of your life – your family, social life, and so on. In this book the domain of principal interest is a job, so we concentrate on "domain-specific" feelings that are job-related – your job-related happiness or unhappiness.

But even within a particular domain (your job, your family, and so on), you can feel differently depending on which aspect you're considering. For example, your job-related feelings can be different about your pay, colleagues or the tasks you have to do. In psychologists' jargon, these are "facet-specific" feelings (about separate facets) rather than being "domain-specific" (covering one particular domain or setting like a job) or "global" (for life as a whole). From time to time it will be important to look at some facet-specific aspects of happiness at this third level of scope, as when "My colleagues are great, but I can't stand my boss." Nevertheless, when people ask whether you're happy or unhappy at work, they're generally thinking in medium-scope "domain-specific" terms – about how much you like or dislike your job as a whole.

The different levels of happiness or unhappiness are likely sometimes to merge with one another. Seeking to work out what makes them hang together, studies have found that people's job satisfaction (a form of domain-specific happiness) is strongly associated with their life satisfaction

Questionnaire 1: Overall job satisfaction

(A printable version of this questionnaire is available at www.psypress.com/joyofwork)

Please indicate below how satisfied or dissatisfied you feel with each of these features of your present job. Circle a number in the appropriate column in each case.

		I'm extremely dissatisfied	I'm very dissatisfied	I'm moderately dissatisfied	I'm not sure	I'm moderately satisfied	I'm very satisfied	I'm extremely satisfied
1	The physical working conditions	1	2	3	4	5	6	7
2	The freedom to choose your own method of working	1	2	3	4	5	6	7
3	Your fellow workers	1	2	3	4	5	6	7
4	The recognition you get for good work	1	2	3	4	5	6	7
5	Your immediate boss	1	2	3	4	5	6	7
6	The amount of responsibility you are given	1	2	3	4	5	6	7
7	Your rate of pay	1	2	3	4	5	6	7

		I'm extremely dissatisfied	I'm very dissatisfied	I'm moderately dissatisfied	I'm not sure	I'm moderately satisfied	I'm very satisfied	I'm extremely satisfied
8	Your opportunity to use your abilities	1	2	3	4	5	6	7
9	Relations between management and workers in your firm	1	2	3	4	5	6	7
10	Your chance of promotion	1	2	3	4	5	6	7
11	The way your organization is managed	1	2	3	4	5	6	7
12	The attention paid to suggestions you make	1	2	3	4	5	6	7
13	Your hours of work	1	2	3	4	5	6	7
14	The amount of variety in your job	1	2	3	4	5	6	7
15	Your job security	1	2	3	4	5	6	7

Today's date:

(global): if you're happy in your job, you'll probably be happy in your life as a whole, and the same goes for unhappiness. That's why we sometimes cover global happiness in this book, although it's otherwise mainly about feelings at work. We'll be as work-specific as we can, but it would be a non-sense to hive off the nonwork world completely.

Similarly, job-related happiness or unhappiness (domain-specific) is mirrored to some degree in narrower-scope (facet-specific) feelings about pay, colleagues and other aspects of the job. In part this overlap arises because the same features at one level of scope also have impacts at other levels; your pay level affects your satisfaction with your job as a whole ("domain-specific") as well as your ("facet-specific") satisfaction with pay. And the overlap between happiness levels also arises in part because of your personality; some people are in general less happy or more happy than others whatever they are thinking about. We'll look in Chapter 7 at evidence that we're all born with a personal baseline of happiness or unhappiness which stays with us wherever we are.

There's another connection between different kinds of feeling. Although people often assume it's important to avoid unhappiness, in fact there are many situations where you can't have happiness without at some point also being unhappy; one is dependent on the other. For example, your positive feelings often come from meeting goals which are personally important to you. But reaching those goals isn't easy when you're doing something complicated, or when you have other problems to cope with at the same time, or when you lack the resources you need. So you may have to feel bad for quite a long while before you have any chance of feeling good; struggles, disappointments and unhappiness can't be avoided if you're working towards a difficult goal. (Writing this book hasn't always been fun!)

That necessary overlap means that often people must work through feelings of anxiety, tension, depression or irritation if they want later to feel happy. (Here, as throughout the book, we're talking about depression in the colloquial sense; clinical depression is of course something else entirely.) No one can be in a permanent state of happiness. Some research has looked at people who are in general extremely happy, recording that even those people often feel bad within their overall happy state. That's why, for example, the founder of the Australian Happiness Institute (which works with individuals and groups to increase their happiness) has his "bad days." Although he's generally happy, he still experiences "times of frustration and anger, moments of anxiety and sadness, interactions with others that are disappointing and distressing."[3]

Indeed, research has shown that negative feelings of unhappiness can have the perverse benefit of making later happiness seem better than it would have been if you'd stayed happy all the time. You can sometimes feel even better because you were miserable before. The contrast between the two directions of feeling as you shift from one to the other can enhance the later experience – a sort of rebound. As we'll describe in Chapter 8, without some contrast you may become adapted to almost any continuing experience so that it comes to have less impact on you. Instead, bad times can sometimes make the good times even better. And of course the reverse also happens – a sudden shift from good to bad happenings can be *really* bad.

Those themes are linked to ideas of "yin and yang," which are central to many oriental cultures. Those describe how opposites (the "yin" and the "yang") are both necessary and complement each other in many aspects of life, such that it's the balance between them rather than the level of each on its own that matters to us. In that respect, research has shown that Chinese people are more likely to accept unhappiness and unhappiness-provoking situations as natural parts of life, whereas (for example) Americans on average seek more immediate removal of unhappy feelings.

You are not alone

None of what has been said so far should be taken to mean that happiness and unhappiness occur in isolation. A lot of people are influenced heavily by others around them, so that their reactions to situations may be partly shaped by a spouse, partner, colleague or someone else.

Daniel Taylor is managing director of Metro Design in London, and he has no doubt his wife Dawn makes a great difference to his well-being – supportive in lots of ways and with a strict rule that weekends are for the family. "I enjoy both work and family life but still find Monday mornings difficult having had a good time with the family over the weekend," he says. "Dawn and I have a united approach to work, we want to succeed but also enjoy the time working. I work very long days and have an interesting life working with my team on large commercial design and build projects. One day I may be putting forward design proposals to the super union Unite, the next day travelling to Barcelona to discuss and oversee a project for the motorcycle company Harley-Davidson and the next looking at plans for the NHS [National Health Service] in regard to building a state-of-the-art emergency response centre." He adds: "Dawn helps to keep me grounded and also to see that work is a privilege and that it enables us to give our children a good life."

These aren't just platitudes, either for Daniel's life or for other people for whom similar rules apply. "When you own a business there are many times like this, struggling to pay the day-to-day bills, dealing with staffing issues, not having the time in the day to do important things, working to an almost impossible deadline – can all play havoc with my stress levels," he says. "Dawn makes me see the bigger picture, talks me through things and I generally calm down. She is also a big help in practical matters. There was an instance when our team of around 30 people were all working nonstop to complete a design installation and all had to go in on a Sunday; suddenly Dawn appeared with a great lunch for us all."

This is a picture of partnership on a personal level. There are other instances in which having the right person to work with in business is crucial. Josh Van Raalte is a public relations practitioner in the UK, and set up his agency, called Brazil, with a partner. He was a seasoned professional and more than able to establish himself alone had he wished to do so. But he decided otherwise: "I am more motivated working with a partner – starting up a business is always hard, and with a partner you are able to find solutions together – both equally motivated and working to a common goal," he explains. "It has helped me focus on the business and not be distracted by outside influences – such as family, especially when working from home initially, as I was. I set up the office in the basement of my house."

But has the nature of the partnership allowed Josh to be lifted out of potentially low feelings about work, which otherwise might have bogged him down? "Many times, working through issues relating to employees, finance, client issues and business strategy," he says. "Dealing with employees has been the most prevalent – and if you have equal interest in a business, you get better feedback."

Interestingly Josh feels that he wouldn't have achieved the same with a codirector, he specifically wanted a partner. "When starting a business, in my mind, it looks better to have two owners, not just one. It wasn't just my motivation, it was the other people. When starting up Brazil, I could have done this myself and "hired" instead of made a partner this person. But I thought that, as a small two-person business, it would immediately create a gap, and also not motivate the other person as much as me – because they would have had less of an interest in the business. If they weren't a partner, I fear they would have had a 9-to-5 attitude, and not gain as much of the business' success as I would have. That's the benefit to me of having a partner rather than a codirector."

These examples of mutual support are presented in this chapter for a special reason. They help us to keep in mind that, although feelings of happiness and unhappiness can be studied in separate individuals, they often depend strongly on others. Recognizing that the people around you are part of your overall picture in these ways, what have psychologists been saying about the nature of "happiness"?

The Happiness Wheel

Much research has been framed in terms of people's "well-being," although that can have several different meanings.

First we need to separate well-being that is "psychological," "mental" or "subjective" (the focus of this book) from bodily aspects in terms of "physical" well-being, although those two can of course affect each other.

Definitions of well-being that is subjective often refer to what New York psychology professor Jonathan Freedman described as either "happiness as peace of mind and contentment" or "happiness as fun, excitement."[4] You can feel good in those two quite different ways – either relaxed, calm and chilled-out, or lively, enthusiastic and elated. Those are both sets of positive feelings, but they're not the same – they differ in the extent to which you're mentally energized or vigorous. Psychologists often refer to that difference as involving mental "activation." Using related words, we can say that people who are mentally activated in that way are more "animated," "emotionally aroused," "fired-up," "high," "invigorated," "keyed-up," "lively," "stirred-up," "vigorous" or "zippy."

So positive feelings of happiness can be either more activated (for instance, in terms of enthusiasm and elation) or less activated (with only a little mental energy – relaxed and contented). And that's also the case on the negative side – being unhappy. When you feel bad, you might be unhappy in an activated, energized, keyed-up way. In that case you'd be anxious, tense and worried. On the other hand, you could be unhappy but lacking in mental energy – lethargic, sad and depressed.

Those four kinds of happiness and unhappiness reflect the feelings shown around the edge of the Happiness Wheel (opposite). The patterning on that Wheel has been confirmed by research studies in many different countries, describing feelings that differ from each other in the two ways just described.[5] From left to right is an axis marked "Pleasure" – how much you feel bad or good. The more your feelings are to the left of the Wheel, the less happy you are.

But your happiness or unhappiness can also differ along the vertical line (up and down), which describes how activated/energized/stirred-up are your feelings; feelings higher up the Wheel are more activated. So the top-right section of the Wheel covers happiness that is

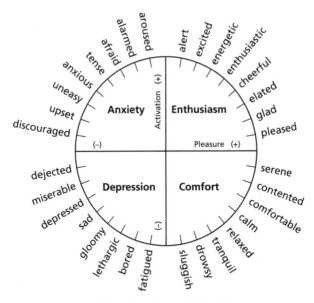

The Happiness Wheel

energized, at the bottom left is unhappiness that is low-activation, and so on.

You might like to think where you're usually to be found in that pattern. Are you generally unhappy or generally happy (to the left or right of the diagram), and is your happiness or unhappiness generally lively or more lacking in energy (nearer the top or the bottom)? And how strongly do you have those feelings? Does your location in the Wheel differ between work and nonwork? Another idea is to consider some people you know; are they in different parts of the circle?

Next, we can simplify the many feelings named in the Happiness Wheel into four basic kinds. Let's summarize those as "enthusiasm" and "comfort" for the two kinds of happiness on the right, and "anxiety" and "depression" for unhappiness on the left. Those four possibilities are shown in the Happiness Wheel by labels in each of the quadrants.

So, back to our opening question: are you happy at work? Rather than trying to provide a single overall answer, you might think about the four main kinds of happiness: which of the four sections best describes your usual feelings at work? And how strong are those feelings? Feelings do of course change from time to time, and you need to pick an appropriate period of time to think about – perhaps covering both the present and the recent past.

If you're happy and you know it . . .

Well, you could clap your hands.[6] Or you might try filling in another questionnaire. Go on – even if you think you are *not* happy. Psychologists have developed and tested sets of items through which people can describe their feelings about work and other aspects of their life. Let's look at job-related happiness and unhappiness in terms of the Happiness Wheel.

Questionnaire 2 covers the four kinds of feeling. You'll see that it asks about *job-related* feelings (in the domain of paid work) rather than your global feelings, about life as a whole.

This questionnaire can be scored to assess several different groups of job-related feeling,[7] but for now let's look simply at happiness and unhappiness – scores on all the positive and all the negative items respectively. In each case, you should add up the numbers (from 1 to 5) of your answers to the relevant items and then divide by six to give you an average score for that kind of feeling. For positive feelings of happiness, combine your answers for items 1, 2, 5, 6, 9 and 10, and for unhappiness combine 3, 4, 7, 8, 11 and 12, dividing the total by six in both cases. See where your two average scores fall along the five response options to give an outline answer to the chapter's opening question.

More about your feelings

As we've said, feelings can be "global" (about life in general) or "domain-specific." Questionnaire 2 can be applied at either of those levels (just change the first sentence in the

Questionnaire 2: Feelings at work

(A printable version of this questionnaire is available at www.psypress.com/joyofwork)

Thinking overall about the past few weeks, how have you felt about your job? Please choose one option for each of the 12 descriptions below. Place a circle around the appropriate number in each case.

	I have felt:	Not at all	Just a little	Quite	Very	Extremely
1	Enthusiastic	1	2	3	4	5
2	Contented	1	2	3	4	5
3	Anxious	1	2	3	4	5
4	Gloomy	1	2	3	4	5
5	Excited	1	2	3	4	5
6	Comfortable	1	2	3	4	5
7	Tense	1	2	3	4	5
8	Depressed	1	2	3	4	5
9	Interested	1	2	3	4	5
10	Relaxed	1	2	3	4	5
11	Worried	1	2	3	4	5
12	Miserable	1	2	3	4	5

Today's date:

instructions), but here we're concentrating on the job domain. Your specific location in the job-related Happiness Wheel is affected by what happens to you in your job. If you're bombarded with unreasonable and conflicting demands, you're likely to feel anxious and tense – unhappy and activated in the top-left section. But, if you've nothing much to do or no sense that your work is worthwhile, your feelings of unhappiness will probably be more in the bottom left of the diagram – unhappy but more depressed than anxious.

There are other differences between different kinds of jobs. Managers are on average likely to have job feelings (both happy and unhappy) that are more activated/stirred-up – nearer the top of the diagram, as either enthusiasm or anxiety. And men and women differ in their average patterns, as women more often express the negative feelings of anxiety or depression than do men.

Notice that we've been talking separately about feelings that are either positive (happiness: like enthusiasm and comfort) or negative (unhappiness: like anxiety and depression). It's often important to consider each of these on its own rather than always combining the positive with the negative into an overall feeling, because the absence of one does not necessarily mean the presence of the other. An absence of unhappiness does not mean that you are actually happy, just as an absence of ill-health does not mean that you're positively healthy or an absence of debt does not mean that you're wealthy.

There's another reason to look separately at positive and negative feelings, and that's linked to the notion of "ambivalence" – having inconsistent feelings about something. As with other important parts of your life, you may both like and dislike your job; work has a lot of different aspects, some of which are less pleasant than others. Writer Studs Terkel introduced a collection of workers' personal accounts of jobs like this:

This book, being about work, is, by its very nature, about violence – to the spirit as well as the body. It is about ulcers as well as accidents, about shouting matches as well as fistfights, about nervous breakdowns as well as kicking the dog around. It is above all (or beneath all) about daily humiliations. To survive the day is triumph enough for the walking wounded among the great many of us. . . . It is about a search, too, for daily meaning as well as daily bread, for recognition as well as cash, for astonishment rather than torpor; in short for a sort of life rather than a Monday through Friday sort of dying.[8]

In more down-to-earth terms, a train driver ("engineer" in the USA) describes his ambivalence like this:

Some people like their jobs and some people don't. I really enjoy mine. I really do. [However] sometimes I don't want to go to work. You know, sometimes I'm, like, oh, God I just don't want to go to work today. I really just want to stay home and be in my own little environment. But there are other times when I can't believe I'm getting paid to do this.[9]

And many readers will understand this worker's outlook:

Frankly, I hate work. Of course, I could say with equal truth that I love work; that it is a supremely interesting activity; that it is often fascinating; that I wish I didn't have to do it; that I wish I had a job at which I could earn a decent wage. That makes six subjective statements about work all of which are true to me.[10]

With mixed feelings of those kinds, it's not surprising that many people find it difficult to decide whether they are happy in their job.

Other aspects of happiness and unhappiness

So far we've concentrated on what are in effect the building blocks of happiness – separate feelings of the four main kinds. As well as occurring on their own, these combine with other themes to create experiences that are more complicated. We've already talked about your work satisfaction, and now we'll look at positive reactions to a job in some other ways – morale, involvement, engagement, self-actualization, perceived meaningfulness, being "in flow," "authentic" happiness and self-validation – as well as negative reactions in terms of job-related stress, strain and "burnout." All of these are forms of happiness or unhappiness, although we don't always think of them with those labels.

Some forms of job happiness

It's noticeable that, although employers and managers are very interested in their own and their family's happiness, they're not sure whether they should be concerned for happiness in their workers. That's partly a question of the difference between "global" and "domain-specific" (here job-related) happiness. Employers might wish their workers a lot of happiness in the global, life-as-whole sense (but believe "that's none of my business"), and at the same time be reluctant to consider the impact of their organization's policies on the same people's happiness at work.

In addition, some employers view work happiness as a rather wishy-washy idea, one which gets in the way of the business's true objective of financial success. Two points can be made in reply. First, worker well-being is unquestionably related to good worker performance; research results have been illustrated in Chapter 1, showing links not only for individual people but also for companies as a whole – staff happiness pays! Second, other labels for the same idea give a very different impression. "Morale" for example.

Almost everyone is keen on high morale in an organization, indicating positive job feelings linked with effective movement towards goals. The term covers feelings mainly in the top-right section of the Happiness Wheel (referred to generally as "enthusiasm"), which feed into behavior which gets the organization where it wants to be. The term is often applied to groups of people, asking about morale in the group or team as a whole.

Research into people and jobs has not often examined morale with its own label, but if you're uncomfortable about advocating policies targeted on how to increase staff happiness, you could instead think of that target in terms of enhancing morale. In that case, positive feelings and good work go together. Even your colleagues reluctant to think of happiness as an organizational goal would probably be willing to look at proposals which can increase staff morale.

Although morale has received little explicit research attention from psychologists, "job involvement" has been studied for decades, asking whether workers feel immersed in their work activities. How much do they agree with statements like "I live, eat and breathe my work" or that "The most important things that happen to me involve my job"? It's usual to let people choose from five responses like Strongly Disagree, Slightly Disagree, Not Sure, Slightly Agree, and Strongly Agree. You're not likely to have an average "Strongly Agree" response to very definite involvement statements like those above, but you could well be in the "Slightly Disagree" or "Slightly Agree" range.

A currently popular version of this idea is in terms of your "engagement" in a job. For that idea, questionnaire items are along the lines of "I get carried away when I'm working," "My job inspires me," or "I'm immersed in my work." It's not surprising that people who score highly on these questions (the ones who are "engaged" in their job) also have high scores on feelings of activated happiness in the top-right section of the Happiness Wheel above. And the connection with "morale" is obvious.

Related themes were popular in the 1960s and 1970s, when American psychologists Frederick Herzberg and Abraham Maslow emphasized people's need for "self-actualization" or "psychological growth," in addition to more obvious concerns for food, warmth, sex and so on. They stressed that many people have a (probably vague) sense that they are not fulfilling their true potential or not being "truly themselves," and Professor Herzberg argued that jobs could and should be better designed to help workers move in that direction; such a change would, he claimed, also increase productivity.

An aspect of this is the perception that doing a job has personal meaning to you or adds to your feelings of self-worth. In such cases, you feel that you are spending your time on activities which make use of your potential, perhaps for the benefit of others. Happiness of that kind is illustrated by Pamela Goldberg, chief executive of the UK Breast Cancer Campaign, when she talked to us about her job:

> If you remember 9/11, I had a call from a friend of mind who's a lawyer a couple of days later. We were working on the edge of the City – there were rumours that London had been targeted as well – and she called and said she envied me, and I asked why. She said, because you know why you're doing what you're doing, and we all came into work this morning thinking what's the point?

An influential idea in this field has been that of "flow." developed and popularized by Mihaly Csikszentmihalyi, based at the University of Chicago but now in California. Flow is the mental state experienced when you are absorbed in a difficult task for which you have adequate skills and a desire to succeed – when you "lose yourself" in it and time seems to race by. Professor Csikszentmihalyi has emphasized how intense and focused concentration in such circumstances can be accompanied by feelings of being at one with your actions and the environment. (He cites as illustrations mountain climbing, chess playing or solving difficult but interesting problems.) In those terms, happiness in a job or elsewhere is a question of frequently experiencing flow as well having other positive feelings like the ones we've been discussing.

Ideas of that kind are central to the currently popular "positive psychology" initiated by Professor Martin Seligman of the University of Pennsylvania in the USA. He developed themes of "authentic happiness," distinguishing between what he called the "pleasant life" and the "good life."[11] The first of those is happiness as we've been talking about it – feeling good and avoiding pain. However, the second sort of happiness, that which is "authentic," was said to arise particularly from the application of personal strengths and virtues, contributing in worthwhile ways to your self-fulfillment. Such activities are less clearly linked to feelings of happiness in the conventional sense of subjective well-being, but they come close to the self-actualization themes introduced above.

These ideas have been developed by another American professor, Tal Ben-Shahar at Harvard University. He defines happiness as "the overall experience of pleasure and meaning,"[12] emphasizing that the "meaning" part is especially important. By that he's talking about the feeling that you are somehow doing something that matters to you, are involved with goals that you really value, and have some sense of self-fulfillment. According to this definition (more restricted than several others), you can experience pleasure (having a great meal, for example) but still not be described as happy, because that additionally requires a sense of personal meaning.

Like self-actualization, the experience of meaning is difficult to describe in everyday job terms, but it can be based on quite minor but personally important activities. So people may be said to be happy in this sense when they are proud of the quality of what they have produced or the help they've given to others, or when they are pleased with the use of skills they've struggled to learn; they feel they have done something worthwhile.

Neither Professor Csikszentmihalyi or Seligman has studied the workplace, and they make almost no mention of happiness that is specifically job-related. However, their ideas appear applicable to some job-holders – primarily those who don't have to struggle with inherently unpleasant jobs and strong financial deprivation. In general we can see how "authentic happiness" can be relevant to happiness at work, but many people are likely to have job concerns in terms of more straightforward kinds of feeling, like those in the Happiness Wheel.[13] Nevertheless, if we want to increase happiness at work, we should think about finding some more "meaning" as well as only "pleasure." We'll look at that in Chapters 9 and 10, when Professor Ben-Shahar will come back into view.

Some forms of job unhappiness

Let's turn now to the negative – some types of unhappiness at work. Researchers and the mass media have contributed to a recent view that people in their jobs are increasingly "stressed." Thousands of studies in many different countries have asked workers how much they feel under stress and what aspects of their jobs they find stressful.

There's no obvious dividing line between being stressed by a job (or "under strain") and merely not liking it, and recent changes in society's norms ("fashions" if you like) mean that it's now often a badge of acceptability to report yourself as "stressed" whereas previously you would have been merely "unhappy." It may be that the apparent increase in stressed workers is at least partly a change in their willingness to describe themselves in that way. Fashion is a very powerful influence.

It's also worth noting that not all forms of stress are a bad thing. For example, sportspeople put themselves under tremendous pressure without complaint, many people like to be stretched by the tasks they have to do, and job applicants regularly describe themselves as wanting to move on to their "next challenge" – in other words seeking a bit more stress than at present. In addition, short-term strain can overall be beneficial (even though it doesn't feel like that at the time) in helping you later to achieve goals which make you very happy. These issues will be explored in Chapter 5.

"Stress" was originally defined as a heavy load (like the stress placed on a bridge by a lot of traffic or by bad weather), but that specific meaning has progressively become expanded (some would say "bloated"). Many things are now described as stressful which in earlier days would have been called merely unpleasant or nasty. Of course, aspects of a job can be negative, but only some of those are truly "stressful" in that they put you under an excessive load.

Another term that's been much overused is job-related "burnout." Originally developed only for staff in personal-service roles (nurses, social workers and so on) who have unceasing contact with clients, burnout questionnaires cover feelings of cynicism about clients and work-tasks and feelings of low achievement – a belief that your activities aren't really doing any good. However, the term, like "stress," has been widely applied in popular writings to refer to almost any negative reaction to a job.

We don't think that such a broad reference is helpful, and we'd rather focus on one particular aspect of the original idea – feelings of emotional exhaustion. Those have been tapped by questionnaire statements like "I feel used up at the end of the working day" and "I feel emotionally drained from my work." There's no doubt that these apply to many people at some points in their working life. When we're asking about unhappiness in a job, emotional exhaustion of that kind should certainly be considered as well as the building blocks of negative feelings introduced earlier in the chapter.

The fact that terms like "stress" and "burnout" can change their meaning to fit with the viewpoint of wider society is linked to a general point. Sometimes happiness or unhappiness is based in part on what other people think. You may have mixed feelings, or you may be unsure whether your reaction can really be called "happy." In those circumstances, when things seem ambiguous, research has often shown that we are especially likely to draw on other people's ideas. Do colleagues think of themselves as happy? Didn't that magazine article say that almost everyone was stressed nowadays? Did I feel like this last week? Why does my colleague always seem happy in the job? Isn't it the case that everyone else is happier than me? (People tend to think along similar lines about money and sex.) So it's sometimes useful to stand back and ask about your job feelings: how far are they entirely "mine" and how far are they influenced by other people's ideas? For example, how would a new arrival (untouched by the local "fashion") feel about the job?

So where are we now?

The first chapters have been setting the scene for a more detailed look at your job and yourself. Here's a potted version so far.

Happiness is universally wanted, in all domains of life. Finding it in paid work presents special problems, because almost everyone has to do a job even if they would prefer not to at the moment and because jobs necessarily require some activities that are difficult or unpleasant. Nevertheless, people in jobs are overall happier than those who are unemployed, and paid work is central to the functioning of almost all societies.

As well as being important in personal terms, job happiness gives rise to good job performance and potentially to organizational success. Workers who more enjoy their job contribute more to it. You can think of this in terms of "morale," which is itself a form of happiness.

Happiness can be referred to in several ways, among which job satisfaction is particularly important. And separate feelings of enjoyment, pleasure and so on are the building blocks of more complex reactions like job involvement. Specific negative feelings like tension or sadness also feed into broader forms of unhappiness.

We've asked you to record your current happiness or unhappiness of those kinds on Questionnaires 1 and 2, and now need to see how those feelings are linked to what goes on in your job. That's the task of the next three chapters.

Notes

1 This questionnaire was developed by Peter Warr, John Cook and Toby Wall, and published in the *Journal of Occupational Psychology*, 1979, *52*, 129–148.

2 See the book by Chris Stride, Toby Wall and Nick Catley cited in Note 7.

3 See page 11 of Timothy Sharp's *Happiness handbook*, published by Finch Publishing (Sydney, Australia) in 2005.

4 See J. L. Freedman, *Happy people: What happiness is, who has it, and why* (New York: Harcourt Brace Jovanovich, 1978).

5 As elsewhere in the book, publication details are provided in the more technical volume underlying this one. See Peter Warr, *Work, happiness, and unhappiness* (New York: Routledge, 2007).

6 The reference is to a children's song, in case you're wondering.

7 The original version of this questionnaire was published by Peter Warr in the *Journal of Occupational Psychology*, 1990, *60*, 193–210. It has been widely used, and results from many studies have been summarized by Chris Stride, Toby Wall and Nick Catley in *Measures of job satisfaction, organisational commitment, mental health and job-related well-being: A benchmarking manual*, second edition (Chichester, UK: Wiley, 2007).

8 From page 1 of S. Terkel, *Working*, revised edition (Harmondsworth, UK: Penguin, 1975).

9 From page 199 of J. Bowe, M. Bowe, and S. Streeter, *Gig: Americans talk about their jobs* (New York: Three Rivers Press, 2000).

10 From page 273 of R. Fraser, *Work: Twenty personal accounts* (Harmondsworth, UK: Penguin, 1968).

11 See the book *Authentic happiness* written by Martin Seligman and published in 2002 by the Free Press in New York. A website providing further details of positive psychology is at www.ppc.sas.upenn.edu.

12 See page 33 of Tal Ben-Shahar's *Happier*, published by McGraw-Hill in 2007.

13 Self-actualization and related ideas have been explored in job settings in the academic text underlying the present book; see Note 5 above. They are there described collectively as forms of "self-validation," an aspect of happiness that is distinct from the more conventional ideas of subjective well-being mainly dealt with here.

4

The Needed Nine features

We left Chapter 3 with some suggestions about the ingredients that matter for well-being, and we'll next build on those to show how you can draw up a profile of your job in the key respects. In this chapter, we'll consider any kind of situation – including a job – and in Chapters 5 and 6 we'll look more deeply into how these general features are important specifically at work.

Sources of happiness or unhappiness

Let's start with a book published by coauthor Peter Warr in 1987: *Work, unemployment and mental health*. This identified what we now call the "Needed Nine" – the nine main external sources of happiness and unhappiness. These are important in any kind of setting, and they create the psychological difference between different settings, for instance having a job and being unemployed or working and being retired. Their labels are like this:

The Needed Nine features in any situation or role
1. Personal influence
2. Using your abilities
3. Demands and goals
4. Variety
5. Clear requirements and outlook
6. Social contacts
7. Money
8. Adequate physical setting
9. A valued role

These features of life affect your happiness in many ways. The first, and essential, aspect of any environment is the possibility of some *personal influence*. In order to gain something positive or to get out of the way of harm, you must be able to make happen some of the things you want to happen. You don't necessarily want "influence" in a big way – running a large company or being a government minister – but you mustn't feel powerless and completely at the mercy of events. This is important for you to avoid pain and maybe achieve some pleasure, but also because it creates a sense of your free existence or "agency" – you're a "real person," not just something pushed around by whatever happens. More positively, for you to do the things that matter it's essential that you have some influence on your world.

Having some influence over events also helps because it means you can change other features in the Needed Nine list to make them better for you and, conceivably, for others around you. For instance, if you're completely lacking in feature number 1 with no personal influence over your life (perhaps you're very ill, or locked into a really dead-end job), you can't get into situations where you can use your abilities (feature number 2) or be exposed to more variety (number 4). And of course your level of personal influence is itself affected by some of the other features. For instance, a lack of money (number 7) means that you can less change the variety of things you do (4) in ways that can make you more happy.

The second essential feature in the list is *using your abilities*. People need the opportunity to apply their skills, doing what they're good at, both to solve problems and achieve goals and also because it's often satisfying in its own right to apply skill and expertise. (Think back to our Chapter 3 mentions of "self-actualization," "flow" and "meaning.")

Everyone has over the years acquired a huge range of behavior that is skilled. Such behavior is often so automatic that we don't realize how expert we are. In other cases, we are more aware that we are applying our own personal knowledge to solve problems in a way that many other people could not do. Being effective in skillful activities is essential for positive feelings about yourself and the maintenance of self-confidence. Take away the opportunity for skill use, and a person can soon become inward-looking and depressed.

Bronte Blomhoj was the Human Resources Director of Innocent Drinks, but returned to traveling the road with the launch of the Scandinavian Kitchen, a café and food shop in London. She was content enough at Innocent and still works for them sometimes, but wanted very much to undertake something of her own. She believes the skills of the people she employs are paramount: "We want to train people so that if they want they can go and form their own businesses later – or not, if that's not what they want to do." Not only do her own people-development skills get used extensively in her new venture, but both she and her staff get to develop new ones.

Third among the Needed Nine in any situation are *demands and goals* from the environment – being required to do something. Although happiness often depends on your reaching objectives you have set yourself, it frequently also comes from goals introduced through your role. Because you're in a certain job, a carer for your family, a member of a sports club, a local councillor or in any other position, you become required to aim for certain goals. And those externally-set goals force you to take action, strive in ways you otherwise wouldn't, experience some obstacles, and maybe make you happy because in the end you achieve something you wanted.

In addition, the process of getting things done can itself be satisfying; "traveling hopefully" is sometimes felt to be more pleasing than "arriving" at a destination. These themes were stressed by US President Barack Obama in his Inauguration Speech of January 2009: "There is nothing so satisfying to the spirit, so defining of our character, than giving our all to a difficult task."

The fourth main happiness feature is some *variety* in your life. Being stuck in one place or doing the same thing over and over again gets people down. That's partly because of processes of adaptation to an unchanging input –we get "used to" things (see Chapter 8) – but also because low-variety settings often lack other of the Needed Nine features: ability use, social contact, and so on. No wonder variety is often called "the spice of life."

Wherever they are, people will resist repetition. The long-running British TV program *Doctor Who* has had many different actors and characters. In one series a new enemy was introduced, called the Master, and he was included as the villain in all 26 stories for the entire year. Writing later in his memoirs, producer Barry Letts regrets that decision to this day: variety was, he believes, essential to maintain the viewer's interest. Although the character reappeared later, he was never again present in more than one or two stories a year.

The fifth of our Needed Nine elements is some potential for understanding what may happen to you. Research has repeatedly shown that having *clear requirements and outlook* is important for happiness in many situations, whereas being uncertain about what to do and being unable to predict the outcome of your actions can bring big worries. This requirement arises partly from the fact that it's essential to be able to envisage possible outcomes if you are to be able to make decisions about what to do next; decisions and plans have to be based on some kind of prediction. Low levels of clarity about your situation and the future can be very worrying, even for people for whom risk-taking appears second nature. Entrepreneurs can rarely be certain that new ventures will succeed but they must stick with them, having no option but to live with the unpleasant uncertainty they have brought upon themselves.

Sixth are *social contacts*. As you know, these are important in lots of ways, and their absence is often a source of anxiety and depression. Interactions with other people are essential for you to develop friendships and feel less lonely, and other people can help you solve your problems and comfort you when upset. Many goals can only be achieved through fruitful working with other individuals. On the other hand, poor social relations with unpleasant or unkind people usually feed into unhappy feelings.

Social contacts are also important to help you to understand yourself better, through processes of "social comparison." Everyone needs to compare their opinions and abilities against those of others in order to evaluate themselves and to form an understanding on the basis of a wider set of views. More generally, it's from other people that you learn what behaviors and thoughts are appropriate in your network; social norms and local fashions affect ideas and opinions as much as they influence clothes and musical preferences.

Another feature whose absence creates unhappiness is of course *money* (number 7). When your own and your family's requirements far exceed the money that you have, it's clear that you may struggle to keep going and escape despair. As well as the problems of paying for essential items, you can't do much to improve other features in the set like variety (4) or expenditure-based aspects of social contact (6). And poverty can be self-perpetuating, as poor people often have to pay more for what they buy, can't afford money-saving equipment, can only pay one bill by leaving others unpaid, and may be stuck with high interest charges on loans taken out to meet emergencies. People with low incomes also have to spend a high proportion of their money on food, leaving little to buy things for enjoyment or fun. Linked to issues of that kind, research has frequently shown that on average distress and unhappiness are worst among poorer individuals.

The eighth feature essential for happiness is an *adequate physical setting*. Everyone needs to be protected against physical threat, and to have reasonable heating, space, and facilities for everyday living. Some physical settings are very inadequate in these respects, and naturally they wear down any potential feelings of happiness. Remember that in this chapter we're talking about life in general, so that "physical setting" means your living conditions – your home, furniture, heating, neighborhood and so on. In later chapters we'll be concerned with the physical setting in a job – your workspace, equipment, safety provisions and similar themes.

Finally, it's important for happiness that you are doing something you can believe in, at least from time to time. A *valued role* (9) provides benefits for other people as well as merely for yourself – as a worker, a parent, a member of a community association, or whatever. For example, recent increases in the average age of many countries' population have created a need for carers to assist older people living at home. Those carers usually receive only low wages, but as one said: "It's all about knowing I can help. I'm doing something that matters to people, and I'll work hard at that." Later chapters will illustrate how this feature brings personal meaning to jobs of many kinds.

Bronte Blomhoj, as mentioned earlier, started her own business in 2007 prior to which she was senior in a major drinks company after working for a merchant bank. She now meets people who view her current position as a step-down from where she was. "I tend to think that's their problem," she says. Her new role assists other people in their jobs and it fits with her own concerns – it's meaningful for her.

Having a valued role is thus partly a question of how you see yourself: are some of your activities personally fulfilling, the kind of thing you think it's worth spending your time on? But, in addition to your own perception, this ninth feature also covers esteem or recognition from others: how far is your role one that is valued in society or in that part of society which matters to you? The two perspectives, your own and that of other people, may well coincide, but that's not always the case. For example, people working in jobs that are widely avoided (cleaners of public toilets, garbage collectors, animal exterminators and the like) can see their activities as socially valuable in many ways, perhaps developing amongst themselves a joint outlook about the positive value of their role.

Unemployment, retirement, home-making, and jobs

That's all a bit abstract, you may think. Indeed it was, because we needed to paint the overall picture. In the next chapter we'll tie the Needed Nine down to job activities: if the features are missing from your work, so is your happiness. First, let's look at happiness or unhappiness in roles outside paid work, when people are unemployed, retired or looking after their family. Thinking about those can sharpen up ideas about what are the important aspects of a job.

Unemployment

How does unemployment look in terms of the Needed Nine happiness features? Not surprisingly in view of what's gone before, people who are unemployed on average suffer in all those respects. Personal influence (feature 1) is low, as unemployed individuals have less chance to decide and act as they wish. Lack of success in job-seeking, inability to influence potential employers, and increased dependence on welfare bureaucracies all reduce a person's ability to affect what happens to him or her. Even a prospective employer dictating the time of an interview reminds you how much you are at other people's beck and call. In the terms used by some psychologists, you are very much a "pawn" rather than an "origin."

Unemployed people's low level of personal influence is harmful both in its own right (feeling powerless is upsetting) and also because it brings an inability to affect other primary features; people can't do much to improve their variety, financial position or physical situation. Reduced influence also arises from other characteristics in the Needed Nine that go downhill in unemployment. For instance, shortage of money (feature 7) stops unemployed individuals from making things happen as they would like.

The second happiness feature, opportunity to use your abilities, is also likely to be reduced during unemployment. People can no longer apply skills in a job, and they usually have little chance to gain new ones. Third, externally-generated goals also decline, as a person is less subject to job-related demands and as purposeful activity is less prompted by the environment. Several investigators have confirmed that unemployed people can have difficulty filling their days, with long periods spent without activity, merely sitting around or watching television.[1] This is sometimes made worse by legislation that requires people to be available for work if they are to be entitled to benefits. At first glance that appears more than reasonable, until you realize it precludes voluntary positions which might otherwise lead to activity and offer some fulfillment.

A decline during unemployment in the fourth environmental characteristic, variety, occurs in part because of the reduction in goals and demands (3, above), and also from a loss of welcome contrast between job and nonjob activities. Experience is also narrowed through the reduction in activity that follows an unemployed person's drop in income.

Aspects of the fifth happiness feature (clear requirements and outlook) are also harmed by unemployment. The future becomes unpredictable in many ways, as outcomes of job-seeking are uncertain and you lack information that's needed for decisions and plans. For example, how will things be in three months time? How do I plan for my family, my home and other important aspects of life? Can I buy this needed item now, or will the money be essential next year? In addition, current role requirements can be ambiguous and confusing for an unemployed person: how should you behave in this unusual situation, how do you relate to members of your family, what do you say to people you meet? Many readers have seen or suffered from problems of this kind.

Relationships with other people (feature number 6) can also take a beating during unemployment, for instance as disputes about limited financial resources play havoc with family harmony or a low income stops you going to social events. Reduced money (feature 7) is another general problem, and a linked shift to financial dependence on other family members can strain relationships even more. Low levels of the eighth characteristic (adequate physical setting) are usually associated during unemployment with low availability of money. The living conditions of unemployed individuals can be really bad, for instance because they can't pay for heating, repairs or replacement items.

Finally, a valued role (feature 9) is clearly lost by enforced joblessness. On becoming unemployed, a person is moved out of a socially-approved position and the positive self-evaluations that go with it. You're no longer a bread-winner and don't feel a full member of society. As illustrated in Chapter 2, unemployment is widely felt to be of low prestige, deviant or second-rate. This is part of the work-is-a-good-thing theme illustrated in Chapter 1. Even when welfare benefits remove the worst financial hardship, there may be shame attached to receiving public funds and a seeming failure to provide for one's family or contribute to society more widely.

In a nutshell, research has confirmed that unemployment creates distress compared to having a job, and revealed that the Needed Nine features are the cause of that difference: the two roles differ on average in those nine ways with associated impacts on well-being.

But of course people are not all "average" and some unemployed individuals are even more unhappy than others. In part that's because different people's environments provide different amounts of the Needed Nine, but also because attitudes, needs, and other characteristics differ from person to person. An obvious difference is in terms of age, and it's medium-age individuals who have been found to suffer the most in unemployment – linked to their requirement to provide for a family and meet its additional expenditure. A colleague of one of the authors was made redundant at the age of 49, and his problems and anxieties about getting a job in middle age added greatly to his unhappy state.

Another factor affecting unhappiness in unemployment is a person's health. Whether in or out of a job, ill-health goes along with greater unhappiness, and studies of unemployed people consistently find greater distress among the ones who are in poor health. All unemployed people suffer from reduced levels of the Needed Nine, but if you're unwell your distress is still greater.

In addition to differences in unemployed people's age and health, it's essential to consider their patterns of motivation. Some people want to have a job more strongly than others, and those unemployed people who are more committed to a job are consistently found to be the most distressed in their situation. (Psychologists often refer to differences in individuals' "employment commitment" here.) Linked to that, many people who adapt to unemployment by gradually reducing their commitment to work come to experience less distress – their lack of a job no longer matters so much to them. (That lower employment commitment also reduces their likelihood of getting back to work – a nasty dilemma.)

So the next question is: why do some people more want a job than do others? It's easy to see that this motivation has two different sources – financial and nonfinancial. (In case you haven't noticed: although we're talking about unemployment, we're also referring to people like you – in a job, caring for your family, or officially retired.) First, some individuals are more determined than others to gain a good income, either because they have a desperate financial need (to meet family requirements or some other commitment) or because they are that kind of person – driven by money to a high degree. A 2008 account in *The Times* newspaper of a sales team meeting quoted the team leader: "All these people want from their job is to buy expensive cars and go on several holidays a year." Other individuals are less concerned about the amount of pay provided by a job, but they almost certainly watch carefully that their income is broadly OK.

Second, nonfinancial motives also play a part. For many people work is personally significant, either for moral reasons or for the psychological and social rewards it can offer. That's not only an individual view; societies develop a collective ideology about work. Chapter 1 pointed to the "Protestant work ethic," which praises the value of working in God's eyes as well as its value for workers themselves, but other societies around the world have their own variations on that theme.

Whatever its basis, commitment to a paid job is a fundamental factor in the unhappiness felt during unemployment: negative feelings depend on how much an unemployed person instead wants to be in paid work. And that kind of motivation (let's give it the general label of a "role preference") turns out to underlie people's happiness or unhappiness in other roles, such as retirement or home-making.

Research studies have shown that those roles affect people in the same ways that unemployment does – depending both on levels of the Needed Nine happiness features and also on motivation to be in or out of a current position.

Retirement

There's plenty of evidence that some people who suddenly retire from work find it a bit unnerving. But many others are delighted by the change. So what is the overall pattern? To locate that, it's essential to match retired and not-retired samples for their age, sex and other characteristics. When that's done in systematic research studies which compare matched groups, happiness turns out to be roughly the same for people who are retired and those who are still in a job. On average, retirement does not affect happiness or unhappiness one way or the other.

But it clearly does matter in individual cases. On what do these individual differences depend? Yes, you guessed. A lot is due to the level of a person's score on the Needed Nine environmental features. Research measuring those has shown that retired people whose life contains high levels of most of the features are substantially happier than those retired people who experience low levels. If your retirement will yield reasonable amounts of money, social contact, variety, personal influence and other features from the list, you are likely to be happy. If not, you won't feel so good. This positive effect is greater for people whose previous jobs were themselves lacking in these ways: life has got much better for them.

Over and above differences between settings, we've seen in the case of unemployment that a person's health and his or her role preference also matter. And of course that's also true for retirement: retired people's poor health goes along with unhappiness, as does their role preference – wanting to be in a job instead of retired.

So we can be quite accurate in predicting someone's feelings during unemployment or in retirement. We can do that by checking the Needed Nine environmental charac-teristics and the person's role preference and his or her state of health. (Try thinking of some people you know.) Of course, there are other contributors to happiness or unhappiness, such as a loving companion or a certain personality, but let's assume for now that those are evenly spread whether people are retired or still in a job.

Home-making

Another comparison much studied by psychologists is between women who are in a job and those who stay at home – a regular topic for newspaper and magazine features. Amid the swirl of conflicting claims, research has made it clear that *on average* happiness levels do not differ between the two groups. Employed and nonemployed women are on average equally happy.[2] There are of course differences in outlook around that average pattern. Some individuals believe firmly that raising a family is in itself a full-time job and should be respected as such, whereas others are a bit negative when someone describes her or his occupation as a housewife or househusband.

Many women are clearly very miserable being stuck at home with their children, but others are blissfully happy. It depends largely on what they want – described formally above as their "role preference." A classic (1980s) study of American married women measured their levels of depressed feelings, finding that those feelings were on average unrelated to people's employment status. Instead, a difference arose from what a woman preferred – staying at home or having a job – in combination with her current position. The general pattern was as you'd expect: people were less depressed if they were in the roles they preferred, whichever that was.[3]

It's not surprising that, if a woman wants a job more than she wants to stay at home, she'll be happier in work. But this points to the fact that overall claims about women in general (as are widely made in the media) don't really help our understanding. It's essential to look at role preferences and to recognize that there's no universal difference between women's feelings in the two roles.

Crucial in comparing the roles in particular cases are the Needed Nine features introduced above. One stay-at-home woman may have high levels of these desirable features in her life – be using her abilities, have adequate money, good social contacts, a varied schedule, and so on. Another woman at home may be restricted to simple, repeated tasks, be short of money and social stimulation, and generally score lower on the nine happiness features.

As the saying goes, "it's not rocket science" to conclude that one of those women will be less happy than the other – she has less of the Needed Nine. Looking more generally, happiness comparisons between different job-related roles (employed, unemployed, nonemployed, retired, etc.) all depend on these nine features. In addition, moderating variables like those introduced above are going to matter – personal role preferences and health or ill-health. When we know about someone in those respects, we can have a good guess at his or her level of happiness. However, personality and other individual characteristics are also important, and we'll look at those in later chapters.

Too much of a good thing?

Some of you may be thinking there's something wrong about these happiness features, because in your case you've clearly got too much of some of them. They're not making you happy, and you want to reduce their level rather than increase it still more. For example, if you go out to work, are struggling with big problems in your job, organizing a family, looking after your elderly parents and trying to juggle events in a social life, you're not likely to want more demands and goals (feature number 3). You'd like some respite.

Research studies have looked at this kind of question, asking whether the key environmental features are increasingly desirable only up to a moderate level. Perhaps they reach a tipping point, after which further increases in their amount (for instance, having still more goals to meet) serve to reduce rather than enhance well-being.

That up-and-down pattern has been documented for several of the nine features. As in the example above, it's established for number 3, demands and goals: you want some (avoiding "underload") but not too many (avoiding "overload"). And it also occurs for number 1 – having some influence over events. Although a certain amount of personal impact on things is essential for your self-esteem and feelings of well-being, if your environment (in a job, at home, or wherever) requires you to make too many controlling decisions you become anxious, worried about making mistakes, overburdened with problems to solve, and generally not happy. Very high levels of variety (number 4) are also of this kind. You can end up with so many different things on your agenda that you can't really concentrate properly on any of them, you can't find time to develop expertise in particular areas (feature 2), and the different kinds of required activities get in each others' way.

So the nine features around you are indeed important for your happiness, but you don't want more and more of them without a limit. In technical terms, this is to say that the relationship between a feature and subjective well-being is not a "linear" one – not a straight-line increase of happiness with an increase in the level of the feature. Instead, the relationship is "nonlinear" or curved. In the examples, above, the pattern is nonlinear in the form of an upside-down U. Starting at a very low level of a feature, as you get more opportunity for (say) influencing your activities you gradually become more happy (moving up the left-hand side of the inverted U). Then with still more personal control your happiness starts to level off, before you slip down the other side of the upside-down U as the requirements for you to control things become more than you can handle.

We'll see in the next chapter what this nonlinear pattern means for job features and happiness, but first there's one more complication. (Sorry, we're trying to keep it simple, but life's not always like that.) Some of the nine happiness features work in a slightly different way. Consider people's need for money. Is the amount people earn related to their happiness in that upside-down-U way?

Money certainly matters a lot when you haven't got much, so increasing your income from a very low level definitely helps. But can you have *too much* money – an inverted U? Research evidence says not; happiness stops going up with continuing increases at really high levels of income but on average it doesn't then go down. Several research studies have shown a stronger association between income and happiness for poorer people than for those who are better-off, but no general down-turn in happiness at extremely high levels of income.

So a lack of money certainly causes distress, and increases in income from a very low level undoubtedly improve well-being. However, after a moderately high level is reached further increases in money have only a limited impact on happiness, and a leveling-off rather than a general reduction is found.

Some lottery winners do become unhappy with their sudden riches, but in general differences between very high levels of wealth appear not to affect their owners' well-being. Money no longer matters on a day-to-day basis when you're very wealthy; other aspects of life become more important in making you happy or unhappy. So this non-linear pattern is one of a strong association between income and happiness across low to medium–high levels of income (more money makes you more happy when you're poor), with money having a more constant importance across high levels (the difference in happiness between having a huge income and an even more huge one is negligible and not in general likely to reduce happiness).

The Needed Nine list thus contains two kinds of happiness feature – some for which extremely large amounts become harmful (producing "overload" and similar problems), and others where very high levels continue to make people happy but where the precise high level of the feature doesn't much matter (as in the case of very large amounts of money). In all cases an absence of the feature causes unhappiness, so that increases in the low to medium range do make for more positive feelings.

However, when people are faced with a very high level of the features, they are likely *in some but not all cases* to become anxious, upset, and more troubled than when only a medium amount is present. These "inverted-U" happiness features are the first six in the list considered here: personal influence, using your abilities, demands and goals, variety, clear requirements and outlook, and social contacts. Although greater amounts of these make you more happy up to medium–high levels, very large amounts are likely to become harmful. Increases in the other three of the Needed Nine (money, adequate physical setting, and a valued role) also bring more happiness up to a medium–high amount, but after that they have on average a constant effect. At high to very high levels, as people get more and more of those three features they are on average similarly happy with no general decrease or increase in well-being.

Readers who take dietary supplements to keep themselves healthy may be sensing something familiar about now. They probably know that vitamins are essential for health but only up to a point. After a certain level of intake is reached, increased doses don't help and may even harm you. With that in mind, "guideline daily amounts" or "recommended daily allowances" have been published for many vitamins. It's rather like that for the Needed Nine and happiness: without them you're unhappy (just as a lack of vitamins makes people ill), but, when your intake has reached quite a high level (like the "recommended daily allowance"), gaining more of them won't help and may indeed harm you.[4] So we'll sometimes be referring to the book's approach as a "vitamin framework." That doesn't suggest you take some tablets, but it does identify features that are essential for a good life and recognizes that ever-increasing amounts of those desirable features can be harmful; there's usually an optimum level both for vitamins and for the Needed Nine.

What about the workers?

OK, but where does your job fit into all this? Issues of happiness and unhappiness in life as a whole can be fascinating, but after all this is a book about work.

True, and the scene is nearly set. This chapter has a general importance: the Needed Nine features apply to all areas of life. Each of your life chunks (for instance your family, your social world, your job) can be described in the same nine terms: they affect your happiness in similar ways wherever you are. However, it's necessary to supplement the general account with additional domain-specific issues for each chunk. For example, a particular theme affecting happiness in the family concerns emotional relationships between partners; that is not generally applicable in all other domains.

For happiness in your occupational life, we need to augment the Needed Nine with three more features that are specific to the job domain. We'll do that in the next chapter. For now let's just mention that the extra three are supportive supervision, career outlook, and fair treatment.

Happiness at work is thus based on 12 principal features – the "Top Twelve." We've introduced nine of these in life-as-a-whole terms in this chapter, considering all kinds of situations. In Chapters 5 and 6 we'll focus directly on work issues, to see how those nine features and the three additional ones have their impact on happiness in jobs.

A quick summary

This chapter has introduced later ones through six main themes. First, happiness or unhappiness in any role depends on experiencing enough of nine main features. These certainly include money, and there's no doubt a lack of money can cause distress and unhappiness. Nevertheless, to properly understand why people feel like they do, it's essential also to consider eight other psychologically-nurturing aspects of the environment.

Second, different job-related situations (being employed, unemployed, a home-maker, retired, and so on) have different mixes of the needed happiness features, and situations' average levels of those features are accompanied by parallel average differences in happiness or unhappiness.

Third, over and above the average pattern, each person's life setting has its own profile of the features. *Within* any role (e.g. comparing two jobs within the employed role) happiness differences between people are largely determined by their personal levels of the features. Thus, a person's chances of being happy in a job depend crucially on these attributes; different people in jobs are differently happy according to their personal exposure to the nine features.

Fourth, the relationship between happiness and the amount of a feature in an environment is not a straight line: ever-increasing amounts won't give you ever-greater happiness. Instead, for some of the features you can have "too much of a good thing." For others, a leveling-off occurs at high levels of input, when still greater amounts of (for instance) money aren't increasingly beneficial. We know which of the Needed Nine are of those two kinds.

Fifth, over and above the nine universally-important features, specific others need to be considered in particular areas of life. For purely occupational settings, three more characteristics are also important. Thus the focus in studying happiness at work needs to be upon the "Top Twelve" attributes of any job: the generally-applicable nine and also three domain-specific features.

These five themes are at the heart of what is sometimes described as a "vitamin model" of the environmental sources of happiness, specifying crucial inputs to life and their "nonlinear" importance.

Finally, there are aspects of people themselves that influence their happiness or unhappiness. We've mentioned differences linked to health and age (during unemployment for instance), and role preferences are also crucial. For instance, are you committed to having a paid job or would you really prefer to be a home-maker? That preference matters over and above your "vitamins" – the happiness features in your situation. Other personal factors such as thinking styles and personality traits will be reviewed in later chapters. Happiness depends on you as well as on what happens to you.

Notes

1 In case you're thinking that these references to "several investigators" or "research" in general are rather off-hand, we mention

again that this account is based on the academic volume by Peter Warr: *Work, happiness, and unhappiness* (New York: Routledge, 2007). That cites more than a thousand research publications in a list across more than 50 pages.

2 It's appropriate to refer generally to people overall being "happy" rather than "unhappy," because that's the usual baseline experience. Large-sample surveys have made it clear that people's average happiness score is slightly above the neutral point – sometimes called a "positivity off-set."

3 This discussion points to the difference between people who are "unemployed" and the wider category of those who are "non-employed." Individuals registered as "unemployed" are by definition wanting a job, whereas a "nonemployed" sample contains those people but also others who are not seeking paid work. Research findings will differ between those groups, although this fact is not always acknowledged in the literature.

4 Research evidence and conceptual implications of a "vitamin model" in respect of happiness and unhappiness are discussed in more detail in the volume cited in Note 1 above. A briefer account can be found in Peter Warr's chapter "Environmental 'vitamins', personal judgments, work values, and happiness" in S. Cartwright and C. L. Cooper (eds.), *The Oxford handbook of organizational well-being* (Oxford: Oxford University Press, 2009).

What's in a job?
1. Seeking a happy medium

Here's a trailer for what follows in this chapter and the next one. We're going to explore the Top Twelve features to see how each one plays its part in making workers happy or unhappy. We'll also highlight some specific aspects. For instance, the third feature in our list covers in general the demands created by a job, but those demands are of many different kinds. So we need also to look separately at certain subcomponents.

Different features and subcomponents are of course more important or less important in different jobs, but you've almost certainly experienced the topics of these two chapters at some point in your work-life. As you read about each one, think about it in your present situation. We'll provide a summary questionnaire later to help you structure your thinking.

The Top Twelve job features

The Top Twelve job characteristics – the ones that most affect your happiness or unhappiness – were described briefly in the last chapter. The box on the next page shows a list of the features as well as some of their specific aspects.

Jobs contain low, medium or high levels of each feature. Some of them are likely to occur together in the same job. So, if you've got a lot of influence (number 1), you'll probably also be using your abilities a lot (number 2). On the other hand, having a low level of variety (number 4)

The Top Twelve features in any job

1. **Personal influence**
   Overall: Having some discretion, independence, or opportunity to make your own decisions

2. **Using your abilities**
   Overall: Having the opportunity to apply skill or expertise
   Aspects: 2a: Using skills that you already have
              2b: Building up new skills

3. **Demands and goals**
   Overall: Being required to achieve job outcomes that are challenging
   Aspects: 3a: Level of task demands
              3b: Conflict between different demands within your job
              3c: Conflict between demands from your work and home

4. **Variety**
   Overall: Variation in activity and/or place

5. **Clear requirements and outlook**
   Overall: Knowing what is expected of you, how you're doing, and what might happen in the future

6. **Social contacts**
   Overall: Interactions with other people
   Aspects: 6a: Amount of contact, irrespective of its quality
              6b: Pleasantness and helpfulness of interactions

7. **Money**
   Overall: Being paid well for what you do

8. **Adequate physical setting**
   Overall: Acceptable physical working conditions
   Aspects: 8a. A pleasant working environment
              8b. A safe working environment

9. **A valued role**
   Overall: Being in a job which is personally significant for you
   Aspects: 9a. Status level
              9b. Contribution to other people
              9c. Opportunity to enhance your feelings of self-worth

10. **Supportive supervision**
    Overall: Having bosses who support your welfare in working well

11. **Good career outlook**
    Overall: Being able to look forward to a good future
    Aspects: 11a. Current job security
             11b. Opportunity for promotion or other positive moves

12. **Fair treatment**
    Overall: Being part of an organization which treats employees and others fairly
    Aspects: 12a. Having an employer who treats staff fairly
             12b. Having an employer who deals honorably with customers, other people and the environment

probably means you're also subject to only a few demands (number 3). Note also that the Top Twelve features can have different importance from job to job, and especially from person to person. People want different things; we'll look at differences between individuals in Chapters 7 and 8.

Chapter 4 introduced the idea of a tipping point in relation to happiness. That is the level at which job features can reach saturation, beyond which additional increases are irrelevant to or can actually detract from happiness. The association between your job happiness and your job's amount of a Top Twelve feature (low, medium or high) is not one of a straight line increase. As we described earlier, the pattern is "nonlinear" in the way that vitamins are good for your physical health only up to a point – up to the "guideline daily amount" or "recommended daily allowance." In very high quantities, taking even more of a vitamin has no further benefit or in some cases makes you ill.

We showed in Chapter 4 how this vitamin analogy works for global forms of happiness about life in general. For example, research findings indicate that increased income (feature number 7) makes people in general more happy up to a moderately high level. However, beyond that moderate level still larger amounts of money don't make much difference to happiness.

This chapter and the next one deal more narrowly with jobs. As for life in general, the first six job features in the list are like vitamins on which you can overdose – you can have too much of a good thing. For example, moderate demands at work (feature number 3) are generally desirable (you don't want to twiddle your thumbs every day) but extremely high demands make you feel worse (you don't want an excessive load either). However, job features in the second half of the list (numbers 7 to 12) work differently beyond the moderately high tipping-point: happiness stays more or less the same as amounts of a feature continue to increase in this very high range. For instance, *extremely* pleasant working conditions (8a in the list) don't on average increase well-being beyond conditions which are merely *very* pleasant.

Six job "vitamins" harmful at extremely high levels

Let's look at the job features in more detail. We'll summarize some research which has measured their happiness impact on workers, and we'll illustrate the experiences of particular individuals. In this chapter we'll consider the first six "vitamins" introduced above – the ones for which extremely high amounts are likely to become more than you want. The other six features will be covered in the next chapter – the ones which have a constant effect once you've reached a level that is "enough."

1. Personal influence

People have a strong need to feel they have some control over what happens to them, and they don't leave behind that general need when they go to work. So it's not surprising that most workers want to have more opportunity to make decisions about their job – how it is done, in what sequence, and so on. There's a lot of talk nowadays about "empowerment" – this is it.

Many research studies in many countries have shown that people's level of job influence is strongly related to their job satisfaction and other kinds of job happiness. Greater influence at work also goes along with greater happiness of a global kind – satisfaction with your life as a whole and generally feeling positive about things. People who describe their influence over what they do at work as moderately high are more positive than others in overall happiness as well as only in their job well-being.

For managers or directors, influence over events at work can of course be considerable. They may control a large workforce and make decisions which affect many people and even the continuation of an organization. But for most of us, personal job influence is of a more modest kind. We may well seek nothing more than some discretion over how our own part of the work is done – arranging some procedures, varying the schedule from time to time, or taking the opportunity for an occasional brief chat.

Technology has helped to an extent, for instance as home-working has become more of an option than before. That's especially the case for managers and professionals, and home-working is valued by many because of the ways they can more influence their schedule and activities. Mind you, surveys have suggested it's sometimes viewed as a way of encouraging unpaid overtime as staff feel they have to carry on until a task is finished.

It's wrong to view workers' desire for some personal influence as an attempt to avoid hard work. There's a lot of research evidence that job-holders take pleasure in being able to improve their effectiveness, both because it makes them feel good and because it helps colleagues also to get their job done. Working well and also having some personal autonomy can be very satisfying.

So, the first feature in our list is really important in determining how happy people are at work. It also has a special impact because it can affect other features in the list. For example, if you have a moderate amount of influence over what happens at work, you are able to affect the timing of particular work demands or better manage conflicting requirements from home as well as work (feature 3b), perhaps introduce some variety when you're bored (number 4), or change how you work with other people (number 6). Look at this the other way around: if you have very little personal influence in your job, you're stuck with all sorts of unpleasant features that you can't do anything about. So of course you don't like the work.

On the positive side, workers' use of their personal influence has been studied in terms of "job crafting." Over a period of time, many people shape their job activities to match their interests and skills. They may informally and voluntarily take on additional tasks which they enjoy (e.g., a shop-floor worker training new colleagues or a hair-stylist advising clients about hair-care) or adjust social interactions or other job features to better suit themselves.

There are obviously limits to what is possible, but the widespread occurrence of job crafting does mean that different workers with the same job title may do things that are quite different from each other. And their success in shaping some activities to benefit themselves can be important in affecting their happiness or unhappiness.

The opportunity to decide on action also extends to decisions about other people. On the one hand, with some personal autonomy you can keep out of the way of people who cause you trouble, and on the positive side being able to involve trusted individuals can make a big difference. Simon Lawrence is chief executive of Information Arts and considers the appointment of his wife to have greatly assisted his job well-being. "I started my business as a consultancy in 1998, and persuaded my wife to help me with the accounts. When I incorporated the company in 2000, I asked her to join the growing team as Finance Manager and she's been with me ever since," he says. "She's learned the job on the job with the help of great suppliers, and although she's not a trained management accountant, she's never put a foot wrong. Most importantly, I trust her absolutely – in all aspects where practical common sense is required. I don't always agree with her, but I respect her honesty and integrity – and I really like the fact that we can share the highs and the lows." Simon's opportunity to make his own appointments was here central to his job and the pleasure he takes in it.

Although we know that middling amounts of discretion at work contribute to positive feelings, we also need to consider very high levels of the feature. Does having to exercise extremely large amounts of control make people feel less good than merely large amounts? Studies have convincingly shown that, as greater levels of influence force people to make many and difficult decisions, job well-being levels off and then gets less for many people. On average, people feel no additional benefit once they surpass moderately high levels of personal influence in their job, and at still higher levels of control they may become anxious and strained, trying to cope with a good job feature which has turned into a horror story. For example, nobody enjoys making colleagues redundant, but to rescue a business it sometimes has to be done – by the person with the control. This downside of personal influence is particularly obvious when you must choose between options that are difficult and when those options are negative. Will you throw 1,000 or 500 people out of their jobs? Which close colleagues will you choose? And what about those other difficult decisions you need to make to keep the company going?

2. Using your abilities

Have you ever thought about what psychologists call "level of aspiration"? The term refers to how high you set your hopes for future success, and was first studied in the 1940s. Researchers showed that, when people are asked to carry out a series of tasks, they are likely gradually to increase the level of the goals they set themselves: they come to aim higher and higher, setting more difficult targets to balance those against their personal level of skill.

As with other "vitamins" in this section, you can aim too high for your own good. A business manager once told us that the least happy people he met were entrepreneurs who kept on wanting to be "big" in business. OK, but what's big? Bigger than you were last week? Donald Trump big? What's big enough? An unattainable level of aspiration can cause many problems.

Nevertheless, up to a point using and stretching your skills can be enormously satisfying. Not only can skilled activity yield success on a task, it is also pleasing as you smoothly run off a sequence of expert activities – doing what you're good at. On the other hand, being forced to leave unused your expertise and skills can be very frustrating – you feel you're wasting yourself. So it's dismal that many workers tell researchers how little chance they have in their job to use their abilities or better still do things which expand those abilities.

Of course, many activities, outside a job as well as in it, become more simple as you develop skilled routines. Some relatively straightforward tasks can't be avoided in life, especially after you've become something of an expert so the activity has become quite simple for you. But to be happy in any role you need to balance those periods of routine, easy activity with occasions when you are stretched in applying your skills to difficult issues. Many investigators have shown that the opportunity to use abilities is one of the strongest factors in enjoyment of a job. In examining the sources of happiness, we clearly need to ask about the level of this "vitamin."

As well as the use of skills which you already possess (2a in the list on page 72), we need to ask about the opportunity in a job for you to acquire new expertise (2b). That is important in two ways, shorter- and longer-term. First, learning new skills increases your ability to handle new problems at the present, and it can make you better at dealing with other key job features – using discretion (1 above), aiming for new targets (3), and increasing job variety (4).

A second benefit of job learning is more long-term. To move into complex jobs you often need to gain new expertise, perhaps with qualifications that are publicly defined. Even if those sometimes seem a bit irrelevant, other applicants for a job will be brandishing their certificates; without one, you're at a disadvantage.

New skill acquisition is of greater significance to younger individuals, who are more likely to want to develop their (longer) future career, and older workers often report less concern for substantial learning. As well as having shorter work-life horizons, older people often report that they are "out of practice" when it comes to learning and they may be anxious that their slower learning progress would make them look silly in contrast to their younger colleagues. Nevertheless, research has consistently shown that workers who engage in new learning come to experience greater job satisfaction than others – whatever their age.

Finally it's important not to overlook – although less easy to quantify – the feeling of self-validation that training can build up in an individual. You've gained something by your own effort, you know more than you did previously, you may be proud of yourself, you are somehow more of a "fully functioning" person. This is an example of the "meaning" side of happiness we discussed in Chapter 3; acquiring new skills can contribute to a feeling of personal fulfillment as well as being useful in practical terms.

3. *Demands and goals*

Third among the Top Twelve job features is the requirement to achieve outcomes that are moderately difficult for
you. It's quite wrong to assume that people simply want an
easy life when they are at work. Undemanding tasks are
certainly attractive from time to time (think of the bottom-
right section of the Happiness Wheel in Chapter 3, see
page 37), but a job goes on unavoidably for day after day
after day. Continuous underload for all those days readily
becomes dull – all work and no play might make Jack a dull
boy, but just watch him glaze over if he gets no work.
Underload also creates unhappiness because it's often
linked to other negative features: little opportunity for
personal influence (1) or skill use (2), low variety (4), and
excessively clear job requirements and outlook (5).

Instead, what you need in a job is a moderate level of
demands (3a in the list). Happiness can come from being
drawn out of ourselves, being introduced to new situations,
and pressed into actions that can turn out to be personally
rewarding. People like to achieve something, even something quite minor in other people's eyes, and seeking to
achieve creates demands of many kinds. Mid-career individuals often report that they want to move to a different
job "seeking their next challenge" – they are looking for
more demands.

Of course, a bigger challenge can bring problems and
hassles as well as positive feelings (as pointed out in
Chapter 3, often you can't have one without the other), but
there is much evidence that as demand level increases up to
a point so do scores on job happiness questionnaires. More
than that, research has also found significant associations
between work demands and measures of *global* happiness,
covering life as a whole.

Notice that goals are connected to each other, so that
achievement of a large goal means being successful along
the way. A substantial goal may be difficult or frightening,
but as you move towards it you pass through a lot of
smaller goals which are more straightforward and can yield
their own pleasure. For instance, on the way to carrying

out a major reorganization (a large and difficult goal), you may have to prepare a report for your boss (a smaller goal); that intermediate task could prove enjoyable despite your worries about the overall target. Although an overall goal may be really hard to reach and the cause of much anxiety, you can get satisfaction along the way through interim success in tasks that are more manageable.

However, this is another feature in life and in a job which becomes a problem at very high levels. Underload (very low demand) is undesirable because it creates low-activation boredom (in the bottom-left corner of the Happiness Wheel in Chapter 3, see page 37), but overload (being exposed to more than you can cope with) is harmful in a different way – increasing strain and tension (in the top-left corner of the Wheel). You become concerned that the things you have to do are too difficult, too numerous, or both.

Aspects of overload have sometimes been studied through the unwanted interruptions that occur in many jobs. Being interrupted in the course of an already heavy-demand job can of course make things worse – unexpected telephone calls, urgent e-mails, technical breakdowns, administrative confusion, requests without warning from colleagues, and so on. Research has shown that in some office jobs almost an hour a day can be lost in that way, not only creating additional hassles and upset, but also ruining personal work plans: the things intended to be done today now have to be added into an already busy schedule at some other time.

Negative consequences of overload are sometimes called "burnout" or "emotional exhaustion" (see Chapter 3). Those involve extended feelings of tension and strain, often with linked physical effects, such as indigestion or sleeplessness and conditions that can remain unnoticed – raised blood pressure, changed chemical levels and so on.

Whatever word and measure you use for its outcome, it's clear that very high demand is likely to be troublesome if it happens too often. Almost all activities aimed at difficult targets necessarily bring you up against overload – it's part of an active and successful life. The goals-and-happiness issue in a job is thus one of appropriate frequency: some periods of excessive demand can be acceptable (with success quite exhilarating – see the interview with Nicky Pattinson later in this section), but extended overload brings about distress. This third feature is another one for which the "happy medium" or the "golden mean" is required.

That brings us to the idea of "flow" – the special experience (introduced in Chapter 3) that occurs when the challenges of a task are substantial but just manageable and when applying your skills gives you a feeling of being "lost" in the activity. People call it different things. An athlete will refer to being "in the zone," for example. "Flow" can occur in many kinds of setting – climbing a rock face, solving a puzzle, playing a musical instrument, or tackling a problem at work. It's a desirable episode of intense concentration in which time races by and task activity seems almost effortless. Although it's not an everyday occurrence, many readers will have experienced this in their job from time to time. It only happens when the level of challenge (an aspect of feature 3) is high and when the high demands match or slightly exceed your personal level of skill. Many people value the experience of flow (although they don't know its technical name), and to achieve it they need to place themselves in settings of challenging demands.

In the Top Twelve list on page 72 we illustrated two specific forms of high demand that often cause problems. One is the presence of demands within your job which conflict with each other (3b). In many settings, different requests from different people require actions which conflict with each other and which can't all be carried out in a given period; or perhaps the successful attainment of one goal means that another one becomes impossible. You can't avoid such an occurrence from time to time, and in examining job content we again need to learn about frequency as well as intensity: does between-demand conflict happen so much that it's causing distress?

Another kind of conflict in the Top Twelve list (number 3c) also concerns two separate sets of demands in combination: the degree to which work activities and attending to your home and family get in each other's way. Time and effort spent at work can't also be devoted to looking after family or home. Not surprisingly, work–home conflict has been found to increase in proportion to the number of hours that you work, so it's particularly common if you have a job that is full-time.

For that reason, many women with children at home prefer to have part-time jobs. In the United Kingdom, almost 50% of female workers are part-time but only about 10% of men. (There's another difference: part-time men are mainly young students or semi-retired older ones, not those of medium ages; however, part-time women are more in the middle of their work career, also looking after children.) More than 90% of part-time British women workers report they are happy with their part-time status – they have found an acceptable "work–life balance."

However, many women are very conscious of the fact that time devoted to home issues can result in reduced success in some work respects – receiving promotion, high pay, interesting assignments, and so on. Like conflicts between goals all of which are within the job (3b), there is no perfect solution to conflicts between work and home (3c). As in other cases, a trade-off compromise has to be made.

Conflicts between the demands of job and family do of course vary between people, depending on other aspects of their job and life. Once again, it's important to look at all the Top Twelve features in your life circumstances. For instance, if you are already overloaded with job problems, then simultaneous demands from home are likely to make things worse, but if your job isn't very demanding you may have more time and energy for your family as well as your job. In terms of positive job features, if your income is substantial (feature 7), you might perhaps afford support through child-minders, house-cleaners and so on, possibly helping you deal with the conflict. However, even wealthy parents can feel conflicted about this issue; some people see the use of a child-minder as a dereliction of their parental duty and even a lack of love for their child.

Work–home conflict also depends on the relative salience to you of the two domains. (Chapter 8 reviews salience and personal preferences.) If you feel very involved in both parts of your life, the conflict will be particularly bad as you try to manage both. However, if either your work or your family are of clearly greater personal significance to you, you might feel better about the situation – happier because you manage well in one domain and aren't too bothered about the other. In that respect, several studies have found that on average men report less conflict between the two aspects of life than do women; you can guess which aspect is usually more salient for them.

Research into job feature 3 as a whole confirms what most people know: a moderate level of external demand is desirable, encouraging action and involvement in issues beyond merely your own concerns. On the other hand, extremely high demands are likely to create anxiety and tension, arising both from requirements of the job itself and from conflict between those and other sections of life.

Finally in this section, let's not be overly pessimistic about the joint effect of different demands. There's often a helpful effect of having to cope with more than one kind of problem. For example, overlaps between work and home can be positive as well as negative. Positive carry-over has been studied in terms of happy workers' after-work behaviors, bringing home cheerfulness and a wish to join in family projects. More generally, contrasts between different settings can be valuable in making you feel even better about both of them; we'll look at contrast effects in Chapter 8.

Nicky Pattinson has run her own business and is now a motivational speaker. She tells her own story, illustrating aspects of the first three "vitamins."

At the age of 39 – and after running a £1.5m [$2.4m] a year business – I found myself on income support after losing a young child (through accidental death at a nursery) and both parents and my home – and my marriage dissolving very dramatically. It's fair to say I was bankrupt in more ways than the obvious – emotionally, physically, devoid of self-esteem and trying to live off £56 a week [about $90].

I spent the next two years trying to survive in a little cottage, bringing up my five-year-old boy alone. Difficult, to say the least!

To be honest, what followed was nothing less than a miracle for me. I met the wife of a business owner in our town. She was intrigued as to how we (me and my husband at the time) had taken a £1,000 [$1,600] a week market stall business to £1.5 million [$2.4m] a year, in just two years. After giving her the intricacies, she asked me to speak to her husband, who in his own words "couldn't find anybody who could sell for anything."

Nervous – never before in my life (or since) have I shook like that! – but the upshot was I started on £16k [$26k] a year and a company car. My son and I hadn't had a car for years.

On that first day – I took what I'd learned from the markets, modified it and applied it to another medium. Cold calling on the phone.

On that first day – I arranged four brand new meetings. From cold. Just using the phone, a list of people and a half-used diary (half-used by somebody else). To put that into some perspective, the previous new-business person hadn't got four new meetings in eight months.

Six weeks later I was sitting in my office, and the boss walked in, clutching a fax. One of those meetings had turned into a £220,000 [$354,000] piece of business. I think I just stood staring at it for ten minutes.

That fax changed everything – it changed things for the business, doubling the turnover in a flick and dissolving any money worries. It changed things for the designers that worked there [it was a design agency and the new client was a household name]. It was very elevating to have household names in your portfolio. But most of all . . . it changed things for ME. I immediately went from the poor broken woman I had been to sales superstar in the eyes of others.

In fact nowhere more so than in my own eyes – I'd changed. I changed enough to do £27,000 short of £1m new business that year [$43,500 short of $1.6m]. Success puts you back together again. It made me alive where I was once nearly dead.

The rest – well . . . a phenomenon. The company was Propaganda – responsible for such brand success as GHD hairstylers and now a multi, multi million turnover company and one of the biggest of its kind in the country.

I went on to other companies and traveled Europe and visited the States, honing my craft. Then someone asked me to speak at a business event and explain how I had taken what I'd learned on a market stall to create millions in revenue for every conceivable type of company.

I'm now a very successful speaker – but to be completely honest, even now when I talk about that day in Holmfirth, all those years ago when the fax came through. Well . . . still makes the voice shake and the eyes well up.

4. Variety

People often comment that "a change is as good as a rest" or complain "I've been there, done that." We like to have some variation in what we do and the company we keep, but all jobs (like any activities in life that recur over long periods) necessarily involve the repetition of core activities: you have to do the same thing over and over again.

The issue for job feature 4 (here labeled as "Variety") is once again to find the "happy medium." You can be happy in your job even though parts of it are tedious and unchanging. A computer-chip worker tells us: "I really like what I'm doing. Sometimes there are parts that are a little boring, but basically I like it . . . It's repetitive sometimes, but so is a lot of work. If I could live my life over, I'd still be doing this."[1]

Research has consistently shown that, if you're stuck with a low level of variety at work, your job satisfaction and other kinds of unhappiness will also be low. That's partly because some change is welcome (the point made above), but also because low-variety jobs are additionally harmful in other respects. For example, repetitive, low-variety work means you have little opportunity to use your skills (feature 2) and your job requirements are likely to be excessively clear (a too-high level of feature 5). It's also the case that when we get familiar with something we adapt to it, so that repeated situations (the ones with low variety) become rather less pleasant than they used to be. (We'll look at that in Chapter 8.)

Workers often find their own informal ways to introduce variety into an unchanging job – forms of "job crafting" introduced under feature 1. They may alter the pace of their work at different times of the day, set personal subtargets as part of an overall task, do things in a varying sequence, seek to be different from yesterday, and so on. Of course, to make those changes you must have some influence over your situation ("vitamin" 1), and some jobs with low variety are also very low in personal influence.

Just as an unchanging job makes for unhappiness, so can variety that is excessive. If your job requires you to change very frequently between many different targets, you're likely to suffer from too many demands (feature 3) and matters can easily get out of control (number 1) as you have to jump from one task to another and some are left unfinished. So it's not difficult to see that feature number 4 needs to be watched, recognizing that repetition can't be avoided and that variety can get out of hand. The "spice of life" can be just too spicy.

5. Clear requirements and outlook

Many people hate uncertainty. Others are more relaxed about it, but in general we are uncomfortable or anxious when we don't have at least a rough idea how things might turn out. In part, this is because unpredictability means we can't plan and decide what to do next; we have no basis for estimating possible outcomes and deciding between them. In ambiguous situations we can become powerless and helpless, and we don't like that.

On the other hand, research has confirmed that extremely high clarity can be a turn-off. When requirements and outlook are completely predictable there's no chance of novelty, surprise or having any personal impact on what might happen. You know exactly what will happen, and you can't do much to change that. You are then like a cog in a machine, simply moving in ways someone else has decided.

This feature's general inverted-U pattern (see Chapter 4) applies also in jobs – you can have either too little or too much clarity. Workers become tense in highly ambiguous and unclear work circumstances and bored when those are entirely predictable and known. You can see why a classic book in this field was called *Between boredom and anxiety* – that's the sweet spot we need to find.

Ambiguity in jobs can sometimes take the form of uncertainty about what you are supposed to do. Many workers report that they are frequently unsure what is expected of them in their role, so they become uneasy and concerned about how they should behave. In those ambiguous conditions it's not clear to you what is wanted and whether you'll be rewarded or punished for something. That kind of uncertainty can be very difficult to cope with. Sometimes the problem arises from inconsistency in your boss or bosses. If your supervisor sends conflicting messages at different times about what he or she considers to be effective behavior, or if different bosses do that, you'll very probably be anxious and worried.

Another aspect of this job "vitamin" is people's need for feedback – learning about the consequences of actions: "How am I doing?" "Was that decision a good one?" Sometimes feedback comes from within the situation itself, as later events make it clear whether outcomes were good or bad, but "success" is sometimes more in the eye of the beholder and opinions about it may differ. You then need feedback from relevant other people – your bosses or colleagues. If they don't provide a benchmark for you to judge your actions by, you are likely to feel uneasy.

Of course, people prefer the feedback they receive to be positive, telling them they're doing a good job. However, personal learning and sometimes organizational effectiveness depend also on feedback that is corrective, pointing to inadequacies and ways to make improvements. There's a difference between "recognition for good performance" (i.e. always positive) and "feedback about your performance" (i.e. either positive or negative), although the two are often mixed up in discussions. In addition to immediate feedback, companies may run a formal appraisal scheme annually or biennially. That's not just aimed at making the company more profitable (although that's certainly an important reason for it); many employees expect to receive information that may help them to self-improvement.

Researchers have found that people unhappy in their jobs often point to ambiguities of these kinds: they may need more clarity about the requirements of their job and/ or more feedback about their performance. When examining good and bad feelings at work, it's essential to consider those aspects of a situation. Some uncertainty is fine (for example, people like to bet about outcomes in cases that are not too dangerous), but once again we have to look for that happy medium.

6. Social contact

The sixth feature in the Top Twelve list can be hugely important. Are your contacts with other people about right – in their frequency and in their pleasantness? As with all personal relationships, you'll have ups and downs, but looking at your job in general do you think your social contacts are a source of happiness or of unhappiness?

Think first about their quantity: how often you are in contact with other people in your job? (That's 6a in the list on page 72.) One set of studies has looked at this in terms of the psychological consequences of open-plan offices rather than traditional separation into smaller rooms. Putting people together in a large single space has clear advantages of flexibility, ease of later modification, and potentially better communication, but research has shown that occupants' opinions are very mixed about the arrangement. In separate offices, people have greater privacy, quietness for concentration, and more influence over when and with whom they will have discussions. In an open-plan set-up, you can't avoid other people, and complaints of too much noise, too many interruptions, and the impracticality of private conversations are common.

You're probably thinking "it all depends," and indeed it does. Different jobs require different levels of privacy or between-person discussion, and (important for this book) different people have different preferences. Recognizing that you can't please all the people all the time, your own feelings about this "vitamin" are the issue for us. Is the amount of your social contact at work too little, too much, or about right?

There is also the issue of the levels of interaction to which an individual is accustomed. One of the authors of this book, Guy Clapperton, takes up the story:

> I spent four and a half years on a trade publication where there was an open-plan office and pretty much constant noise. After that, going into freelancing was a shock as there was only me and the two cats. I got used to this and then was asked to write some news in another office a couple of years later. So I turned up and everyone was bemused to watch me waiting for a bit of quiet before I started. Of course, in a busy office there would by definition be no bit of quiet for me or for anyone else.
>
> The punchline, I suppose, is that the next time I visited my old office I found they'd put up a soundproof wall to keep the noise out from the other magazines working on the same floor. Odder still, although they were now working more effectively and they were happier, to a lot of other magazines they'd undermined their credibility and become some sort of running joke. This niggled them more than somewhat.

Like the other "vitamins" in this chapter, continuing close social contacts can become oppressive and a source of irritation. One contact told us how he found himself pressed into a "bowling evening" with some customers on one occasion. He wasn't familiar with the American model of bowling alleys which are popular in the UK and he and a number of colleagues were not only uncomfortable with putting on shoes that had been worn by others in order to play, but then found themselves the butt of jokes among the others because they hadn't done this sort of thing before.

Societies throughout the world have created structures and ways of living together that maintain the advantages of social contact but also control against overcrowding and to permit privacy. In the bowling incident, clearly it broke down. When you think about it, it's remarkable that people manage the same social contacts in the workplace for so long. That is the only environment in which individuals are put together on a continuous basis with others for whom they haven't a family relationship or the right to select their company.

The second aspect (6b) of this "vitamin" is of special significance to many people – the pleasantness of inter-actions. Many workers report that other people are the main source of their unhappiness at work. The concern is usually with colleagues who are unpleasant, but of course some workers have to deal also with clients and other members of the public, and those too can cause difficulties. Telephone call-center staff, bus drivers, some shop assist-ants, and even nurses frequently describe insults, criti-cisms and generally hurtful treatment from people they deal with.

In some cases, the issue is simply that you don't like the people you meet. That can happen outside a job as easily as inside one. However, the problem isn't always a clash of personalities and styles; it can arise from persistent unkindness, bullying, abuse or harassment. Those harmful low levels of the "vitamin" can occur without conscious intention, or they can be purposeful insults, social exclu-sion, offensive e-mails, malicious gossip, or other forms of humiliation. A colleague of one of the writers spent a lot of the early 1990s having his dress sense and weight laughed at in an office. The ridicule was perhaps intended in good part but it added to low morale and poor performance and would be unlikely to be tolerated now.

On the brighter side, positive forms of social contact are widespread at work. People can enjoy talking together about work or nonwork issues, can share useful ideas about how to solve practical or personal problems, and generally provide and receive the support that is essential in everyone's life. Studies examining the sources of job satisfaction have often pointed to the impact of colleagues. In some cases work-mates provide important but localized benefits like "keeping me sane in this place," but it's clear that more substantial friendships can also grow from working together.

Can beneficial social contacts be excessive? Research suggests that indeed they can. For example, although it's pleasing to receive help from colleagues as you do your job, it can become exasperating if they persist in offering help when you don't really need it. Or you may grow tired of the work-mate who repeatedly stops by for a chat. Although support from other people undoubtedly enhances job well-being, it can become over-the-top, too much of an interruption, or plain patronizing. Once again, it's possible to have too much of this good thing.

Social needs can also change according to the other circumstances in an employee's life, as we have already discussed. A colleague joined a consumer magazine after working in isolation for some time. He felt the opportunity to slip over the road for a quiet beer or four with his colleagues was an excellent thing after work during the early part of that employment. By the time he left he was a married home-owner and more inclined to go back to the place of his choosing rather than of his employment; the pressure to join in and "come over the road for a drink" was less welcome.

A quick review

In this chapter we've been looking at the first six of the Top Twelve happiness features in jobs – the ones for which you can have "too much of a good thing." We've listed them like this:

1. Personal influence.
2. Using your abilities, with two elements deserving attention: using current skills and acquiring new ones.

3. Demands and goals, with three elements to examine: overall level, conflict between demands in your job, and conflict between job and home.
4. Variety.
5. Clear requirements and outlook.
6. Social contacts, with two elements: amount and pleasantness of interactions.

There's a lot of research evidence – and a lot of personal experience – telling us that these six features make a big difference to happiness or unhappiness in jobs. Particular problems arise if they occur at low levels (like a vitamin deficiency), but it's also possible to suffer from excessively high levels (like a vitamin overdose) – having too much of a good thing.

Later we're going to focus on aspects of your own job, and we'll look again at these features as you yourself experience them. At that point we'll need also to consider the other members of the Top Twelve – they're in the next chapter.

Note

1 See page 106 of J. Bowe, M. Bowe, and S. Streeter (eds.), *Gig: Americans talk about their jobs* (New York: Three Rivers Press, 2000).

What's in a job?
2. When enough is enough

The "vitamin model" proposes 12 features as the primary sources of job happiness and unhappiness. As we said in Chapter 4, the first nine of those are crucial in any setting. All the features are harmful at low levels – similar to a deficiency of vitamins – and numbers 1 to 6 (considered in the last chapter) are also harmful at very high levels – like high intakes of vitamins that are toxic. The remaining six have on average a constant effect on feelings after a moderately high threshold has been reached. In those cases, further increases across levels of a feature which are already high and beneficial don't provide additional benefit – you've already reached a plateau of what is "enough."

Six more job "vitamins"

Let's now look at these six "constant effect" job features: the ones for which low levels make people unhappy, moderately high levels make them happy, and extremely high levels don't create happiness beyond that of the moderate levels. Sticking with the Top Twelve list as presented on page 72, the next one is number 7.

7. Money

Many people consider their income level to be a top priority: they very much want to earn a lot. Here's a self-employed cleaner of crime scenes in the USA, dealing with the mess after murder and other physical brutality. It's clearly a very nasty and gruesome job, but "my goal is wealth, bottom line . . . I want to be bodyguard rich – so rich that I need a bodyguard wherever I go. I'd like to be able to do whatever I want, at any time. If I use a helicopter to go somewhere, I want to buy that helicopter. That's the kind of wealth I'm talking about. And I'm going to achieve it or die trying."[1]

Of course a good income can make you feel good without that level of determination. It can pay for the necessities of life and also provide for luxuries and additional pleasures. However research in many countries (see Chapter 4) has shown that, once you've reached a moderate level, still-more income doesn't make you feel even better, apart perhaps from an initial good feeling.

There are many studies and real-life examples to back this up. In 2004 American psychologists Allen Kanner and Tim Kasser edited a book called *Psychology and consumer culture: The struggle for a good life in a materialistic world*.[2] "When money becomes the focus of what you think is important, your motivation and well-being suffer," said Kasser at the time of the launch. "Increases . . . in one's salary don't equate with increases in happiness." The study came about when Kanner found that children with behavioral problems were coming to him with changed ambitions. They used to want to be baseball players, ballerinas, astronauts, you name it, but now they came saying they just wanted to be rich. The issue wasn't just about children. The book's review of studies with adults concluded that the pursuit of money for its own sake was undermining rather than enhancing happiness. Many overworked individuals were exhausting themselves in the search for even more money, aiming to sustain or exceed their extravagant style of life and harming themselves and those around them.

None of this is to say that a lack of money is positive. We can argue about what is "moderate" in terms of income (around the national average? about the same as your friends? a bit more than you had before?), but it is clear that there is a financial tipping point for happiness. Below that point, the size of your income makes a big difference to your feelings (both in a job and for happiness that is global), but at higher levels of income there isn't much of a link. And for some people who have successfully battled to become rich, a pressing question can arise: "What do I do now?" They need to find other goals and motives, and that's not easy after years devoted only to money-making.

So we need to amend the common suggestion that "money can't buy you happiness." It can do that when you are poor, but for well-paid workers other themes in the Top Twelve are more important. If you are reasonably well-off and you aim only for money, that usually won't make you happy, and things can go wrong with the other 11 requirements. In assessing your job, income level is only one of the bases of happiness. Once you're "comfortable," you especially need to look at other aspects.

8. Adequate physical setting

Another source of many grumbles as well as occasionally of pleasure is the physical setting of work. The list on page 72 pointed out two separate aspects of this: the pleasantness of an environment (8a) and its safety in terms of physical hazards (8b). It hardly needs saying that low levels of those aspects give rise to feelings that are negative.

There are of course extreme sports and other activities in which a lack of safety is a key part of the appeal. At the time of writing, the BBC in the UK was running a radio series reuniting mountaineers such as Sir Ranulph Fiennes with the people with whom they shared their expeditions; clearly nobody wanting comfort and safety would ever have embarked on one of these trips. However, research with "ordinary people" confirms what you'd expect: unpleasant or unsafe working conditions cause dissatisfaction in most jobs.

It also seems likely (but remains unresearched) that as conditions get progressively better a tipping point is reached, beyond which further increases in pleasant features or safety levels have no additional attraction. Bad or unsafe conditions are undoubtedly troubling, but improvements to already-good conditions probably don't make a great deal of difference.

You can see by now that features in the Top Twelve are not all of equal importance. For instance, "vitamin" 1 (being able to influence what happens to you) has the greatest effect on happiness ("morale" if you like, as described in Chapter 3), whereas having pleasant working conditions (8a) may be less influential. In part, this is a question of the level available to you: when it is extremely low (your working conditions are really terrible, for instance), a feature is likely to be of special concern, whereas you don't much bother about it when it's in the "OK" range.

There are also differences between people. Some people are fussy about the quality of their surroundings, whereas others don't greatly notice them; some are obsessive about being careful, whereas others take risks to the point of foolhardiness. That applies generally. For example, some individuals (the extraverts among us) view frequent social contacts ("vitamin" 6) as essential for happiness, whereas more introverted people are less bothered about that. Personal wants and preferences of those kinds will be covered in Chapters 7 and 8.

9. A valued role

Your impressions of people are often based on the nature of their occupation. Answers to the question "And what do you do for a living?" can be important in forming ideas about them. We also think of ourselves in those terms. Job happiness can require some fit with doing what is valued in your society – the ninth characteristic to be considered here.

In some cases, a judgment of a job's value may be made in terms of hierarchical position – your visible status in a group or society at large – but the judgment can also be a more individual matter concerned with your own self-esteem. Page 72 thus suggested three components of the overall feature: status level, contribution to other people, and the opportunity to enhance your feelings of self-worth.

The first of those (9a) reflects your social position – where do you fit in relation to other people? Individuals often find ways to describe themselves in positive job terms.

For example, you may exaggerate a bit the glamour of your job title, and if you're unemployed it's comforting to say you are a whatever-you-were-before. Social roles often have associated clothes, uniforms or other features to indicate their presumed status, and it's widely found – and not very surprising – that many people in low-status jobs would like to see themselves in more respected roles. (Of course, that's partly because higher-status jobs can also have other attractive features in the Top Twelve list.)

Another aspect of a job's personal importance is the opportunity to make some contribution to other people (9b). Helping others is an obvious source of satisfaction to many job-holders in the caring or charitable sectors, but it can also affect many other people's work feelings. Dr Adam Grant of the Wharton School of Business in Philadelphia, USA, has made a special study of this topic. He cites a fire-fighter: "Why do I risk my life by running into a burning building, knowing that at any moment . . . the floor may give way, the roof may tumble on me? . . . I'm here for my community, a community I grew up in, a community where I know lots of people."[3]

Feelings like that are important for many people's happiness at work. An Alaskan fisherman provides an extreme example. He is excited that "there's this electric feel [around here] . . . You fish, and the whole town revolves around you . . . You are responsible for the whole town. If your job is erased, then the town will be erased."[4] A less dramatic social value, more like that experienced by many readers, was described by a builder like this: "I find [my job] very rewarding. Just building something, creating something, and actually seeing your work . . . You start with a bare, empty lot with the grass growing up and then you build a house. A lot of times you'll build a house for a whole family, and you see them move in; that's pretty gratifying."[5]

Many workers can shape their activities and time allocations to some extent (that's "job crafting" described earlier in respect of "vitamins" 1 and 3), so that their adjusted role allows them to feel better for supporting or assisting others in some way. Of course there are limits to that kind of adjustment, but research has revealed that it's much more widespread than you might expect. Some workers develop a greater social value in their job by shaping it informally to allow more help to other people – clients, customers or colleagues.

As with other job features, individuals differ in the personal salience they attach to having a role that is socially or personally valued. Another way of looking at this is as the opportunity to enhance your self-worth (9c) – the feeling that a job fits with your image of yourself and contributes to personally-fulfilling goals. This can be a question of religious or social morality, or it can be entirely of your own making as you seek to be the kind of person you want to be. One woman describing her job was very clear: "Whatever you do, I've always taught my kids . . . you're doing it for yourself. You have to respect your work . . . [My present] job is no more meaningful than any other job except it means something to me."[6] Think back to the definitions of happiness in Chapter 3. Some of those involve more than just experiencing pleasure, they also cover a sense that you're doing something that's personally worthwhile.

Some research has asked workers whether they view their job more as a "calling" (being personally and socially fulfilling) or more as a "job" that needs to be done as a matter of necessity. Even within the same role, there are sharp differences between people in that respect. Some workers see themselves in a calling, whereas others (even with the same job title) see themselves as merely doing a chore; and many view their position as a mixture of the two.

The personal importance of this "vitamin" also varies between people in other ways. If your job is seriously lacking in other key features, you may be particularly concerned about those and less bothered about feature 9. On the other hand, if you're generally OK in other respects (they've reached the "enough" level), you may feel able to take a look beyond the basic requirements. Individuals who pause to ask themselves "What am I doing with my life?" are drawn to think about this "vitamin" – "Is my work worthwhile?" It's clearly essential to measure the presence or absence of feature 9 through job-holders' own views, rather than seeking objective indicators; those are very hard to find and can't apply identically to everybody.

10. Supportive supervision

We're nearly at the end of this review of possible job influences on your happiness or unhappiness. "Vitamin" 10 is widely important, often being the topic of comparisons and grumbles when groups of staff get together – their boss.

Research has pointed to two main aspects of good leadership, described as "initiating structure" and "consideration." You might like to think of your boss in those terms, or (if you're in a leadership role) consider where you are placed. First, good bosses need to create and monitor adequate "structure" in a situation – specifying goals and timetables, allocating tasks, providing information and resources, and generally making things happen in an effective way. Second, the good supervisor does those things in a "considerate" manner – showing concern for subordinates' welfare, listening to and accepting suggestions, expressing appreciation for work well done, and so on. Earlier in the book, food-shop owner Bronte Blomhoj spoke about making her employees feel wanted and a part of something; that's an example of what we're talking about here.

These two aspects of leadership don't necessarily go together. A boss can be good in one respect but poor in the other. This separation into two types of good behavior occurs in many different roles, and can be described generally as professional expertise (analogous to "initiating structure") in conjunction with "socio-emotional" behavior, similar to "consideration." Think of doctors: they may have a wonderful "bedside manner" but that doesn't necessarily mean they're technically competent. It's clearly important to look at both aspects.

We've put the two together in our definition on page 72 of key feature 10: having bosses who support your welfare in working well. It's obvious that people like to have bosses who are nice to them, but niceness needs to go along with getting things done. A "good boss" isn't the same as a good friend – both may be supportive, but supervisors also have their job to do. So the positive boss behaviors we're focusing on are the ones that combine supportiveness with effectiveness.

As in other cases, there is evidence for the importance of this feature at the level of entire organizations as well as for individual workers themselves. A recent British study recorded the average job satisfaction of members of different companies. Some of those had an overall level of worker satisfaction much greater than others. Why? A particularly strong predictor was the average amount of supervisory support that was available: companies with more supportive bosses also had greater average levels of job satisfaction.

The boss behaviors involved in feature 10 are similar to those introduced under "vitamin" 6b above – the pleasant-ness or unpleasantness of social interactions. So stories of very unsupportive bosses can be similar to tales of poor interpersonal relations in general. They may concern hurt-ful comments, bullying, insults and harassments, but in addition for bosses we need to consider unpleasant treat-ment linked to their formal power – favoritism, belittling staff, shouting at people, blaming them for problems they did not create, punishment that is inconsistently applied, and so on.

Note also that a boss's behavior doesn't only have an immediate impact on feelings. It also makes a difference to other key features in the Top Twelve. Circumstances vary, but to differing degrees supervisors' decisions can deter-mine, say, how much you use your abilities (feature 2), the demands and goals you face (3), or your pay level (7). Not surprisingly, bosses can have a strong impact on people's feelings about their job.

11. Good career outlook

In the Top Twelve summary on page 72 we described "vitamin" number 11 as "being able to look forward to a good future," and suggested two principal aspects: your current job security (11a) and your opportunity for promotion or other positive moves (11b). As with other features in this section, these are of major (harmful) importance when they are absent or low; beyond moderate levels their positive value is likely to remain about the same.

Research has often documented the high levels of tension and anxiety that accompany raised job insecurity (a low level of 11a). Even though a person still has a job he or she has a lot to worry about, and insecurity can be painful throughout a family, as one or more members see that their job is under threat. (Related issues of unemployment have been covered in Chapter 2.) It's clear that this is a key element in the sources of job feelings. As we write this chapter, major economic problems are filling newspapers and radio and television programs with stories of worried people concerned about the consequences of losing their job. In other financial circumstances those concerns are much less pressing.

A second element of "vitamin" 11 is the opportunity for attractive moves in the future. Being stuck, with no prospect of shifting in a desirable direction, can nag away at people, but unsatisfactory situations may be tolerated if you see that they can lead to something better. More positively, many people are looking for a sense of progression in their lives.

It's often the case that they are looking for promotion up a career ladder so that jobs are evaluated in terms of potential upward movement – in the present or a different organization. However, other possible futures can also be attractive – sideways movement to do something different, down-shifting to reduce excessive burdens, or a move into a more socially-oriented role, helping disadvantaged people or making ecological contributions to "saving the planet." Other domains in someone's life can be important, too. A library assistant we know accepted a job with little prospect of promotion explicitly because it allowed her to keep up with her family life. That was her idea of a Good Career Outlook. She was not career-oriented in the traditional sense; for her, a good career balanced work and family.

In assessing a job in respect of feature 11 we thus need to think about several themes. A person's feelings in this area depend on his or her family position, age and personal aspirations, but they can often usefully be brought together into an overall, summary assessment.

12. Fair treatment

People have a wide-ranging concern for fair and equitable treatment in life. They notice whether people are dealing with each other in an honest and appropriate way. As part of that, many workers attach particular importance to their company's treatment of individuals and the environment in general – is that fair and honorable? As in other cases, it is often low values (unfairness and inequity) that receive particular attention.

In the list on page 72, we identified two directions of fair treatment – internal and external to the organization. In respect of internal fairness, research has often shown what we know from personal experience: organizations that are unfair in their treatment of employees (other people as well as ourselves) are widely viewed as undesirable places to work. At issue here are biased allocations of "good" jobs or pay, favoritism in granting rewards, possible discrimination in terms of sex, age or other personal features, and generally a departure from an acceptable moral code. There are many possible forms of unfairness, and most of us have experienced some of them from time to time.

Injustice at work creates dissatisfaction both in its own right and also because it may be accompanied by harmful levels of other "vitamins." For instance, within-company injustices (deficiencies of "vitamin" 12a) often go along with abusive supervision (a low level of feature 10) or lead to unfair allocations of other desirable features within the Top Twelve. Coauthor Guy Clapperton has edited several editions of *Britain's top employers*, and was aghast one year to learn that a candidate company forced people to take sick days out of their annual leave. "It makes them get better quickly" was their explanation.

The second aspect of this feature (12b) is a concern for ethical issues outside the organization. Linked to a growing awareness of "green" approaches to the environment, worries about global carbon warming, unhappiness about wastefulness (think plastic packaging), waste recycling and similar issues, a company's "social responsibility" is increasingly under the spotlight. (As an aside, the company which made people take sick days as annual leave was wholly committed to its local environment, for example paying for the painting and upgrade of the local train station.)

Related themes can concern the adequacy or inadequacy of conditions in suppliers' workshops, perhaps those in far-away countries. Every now and again, conditions of work are treated with delight by a newspaper which has discovered an alleged failing by an otherwise respected company. And marketing consultants and others have picked up people's concern for this area to develop and promote favorable company "brands" based on justice and morality as well as product or service quality.

In cases where an organization is clearly irresponsible in terms of feature 12, many employees will be uncomfortable, perhaps irritated, and (if one is directly involved) anxious. Injustice is sometimes handled by leaving the organization. At the other (front) end of the employment process, it has been shown that people looking for a place to work often choose future employers on the basis of an apparent match with their own personal values. It's sometimes said that "the people make the place," but to some extent also "the place makes the people," as it draws in staff with its own set of values.

There are undoubtedly wide variations between individuals in the level of their concern for this issue. Some people have a stronger sensitivity to equity issues in organizations than others, being particularly troubled by deviations from high standards in that domain. Other people, while behaving morally in their own life, don't give much thought to ethical issues in the area of work – they just get on with it. For the purposes of this book, it's clearly essential to examine your personal perspective rather than applying seemingly-universal standards of equity.

The general idea

Let's run through the key points in Chapters 5 and 6. The Top Twelve job features have been shown in research studies to underlie happiness and unhappiness at work. In all cases, low levels of a feature are harmful and moderately high levels are desirable. The first six features (see the list on page 72) are also troublesome at very high levels; in those cases you can have too much of a good thing.

These 12 characteristics of a job are similar in their impact on happiness to vitamins in their effect on physical health. Too small an intake (a "deficiency") is unhealthy and a "guideline daily amount" is good for you. Very high levels of a feature can become "toxic" in the first six cases, and they don't yield extra benefits for "vitamins" 7 to 12 (the ones in the present chapter) once you've reached the level that is "enough."

Different jobs have different amounts of the key features, and those differences substantially account for differences in workers' job satisfaction and other aspects of their happiness or unhappiness. We've not mentioned this previously, but different types of organization have their own patterns of some of the features. For example, the formality of large bureaucracies can be reflected in low personal influence (feature 1) and in task requirements that are extremely clear (number 5). Small companies (which are often found to be the happiest) are likely to provide considerable personal influence, skill use, and variety (features 1, 2 and 4), since their lack of technical and personnel specialists means that staff more often have to solve their own problems instead of handing them over to someone else.

The 12 features are not of equal importance in all settings. Some differences in impact arise from the actual level of feature: when it is extremely low or problematically high, it matters more to you than when it is at a comfortably moderate level. Features' importance also depends on a person's preferences and wants. For example, some people like to have a large number of social contacts (6), others are very concerned about organizational fairness (12), and still others are very keen to earn a fortune (7). Differences of those kinds will be reviewed in later chapters.

Ticking the boxes

Let's now think about your own job. Questionnaire 3 on the next two pages is a simple questionnaire covering the Top Twelve features. At this stage, each one is treated overall, for example lumping together different aspects of Demands and Goals (3) or of Social Contacts (6). However, if some of the specific aspects shown on page 72 are particularly troubling you (such as conflict between task demands [3b] or between work and home [3c]), please also think about those as extra items in the questionnaire. The work aspects are listed under their Top Twelve labels, with a few words of explanation. However, it's difficult to summarize some of them in the space available, so don't forget the more detailed account that has been given in the text.

Thinking about your job in the past few weeks, how would you describe it in these 12 ways? Are any of the features at a level below 4 in the questionnaire? And what about scores of 6 and 7 on the first six of them? In those cases, you might like to start thinking about what changes could possibly be made. We'll suggest a more detailed procedure in Chapters 9 and 10, when we look at steps that you can take to increase work happiness.

For now, we'd like to emphasize that your job feelings can probably be traced back to some combination of the 12 features and their subcomponents. However, there's more to it than that; a principal theme of the book is that the environment (for instance your job) doesn't determine happiness or unhappiness on its own. Your own characteristics also come into it. Could it be that you were born unhappy or that you think in ways which make you feel worse? Stay with us into the next chapter.

Questionnaire 3: Features in your job

(A printable version of this questionnaire is available at www.psypress.com/joyofwork)

Considering all aspects of your job in the past few weeks, please summarize that by placing a circle around the appropriate number in each case below.

		The amount of the feature available to me is:					
	Very much too low	Much too low	Slightly too low	About right	Slightly too high	Much too high	Very much too high
1	Personal influence (What you can change)	1	2	3	4	5	6	7
2	Using your abilities (Applying your strengths)	1	2	3	4	5	6	7
3	Demands and goals (What you have to do)	1	2	3	4	5	6	7
4	Variety (Different activities)	1	2	3	4	5	6	7
5	Clear requirements and outlook (Not too much uncertainty)	1	2	3	4	5	6	7
6	Social contacts (Enough and good dealings with others)	1	2	3	4	5	6	7

		Very much too low	Much too low	Slightly too low	About right	Quite acceptable	Very acceptable	Extremely acceptable
7	Money (Getting paid)	1	2	3	4	5	6	7
8	Adequate physical setting (Working conditions)	1	2	3	4	5	6	7
9	A valued role (Social consequences and self-worth)	1	2	3	4	5	6	7
10	Supportive supervision (Helpful in getting the job done)	1	2	3	4	5	6	7
11	Good career outlook (Security and prospects)	1	2	3	4	5	6	7
12	Fair treatment (For employees and others)	1	2	3	4	5	6	7

Today's date:

Notes

1 See pages 102–103 of J. Bowe, M. Bowe, and S. Streeter (eds.) *Gig: Americans talk about their jobs* (New York: Three Rivers Press).

2 Published in Washington DC by the American Psychological Association.

3 From Adam M. Grant's "Relational job design and the motivation to make a prosocial difference" in *Academy of Management Review*, 2007, *32*, 383–417.

4 See page 221 in the book referenced in Note 1.

5 See page 36 in the book referenced in Note 1.

6 See pages 42-43 in the book referenced in Note 1.

It's in your genes as well as your job

We've all met people who seem to be continuously gloomy – unhappy in what they say and do, and generally emphasizing difficulties and problems around them. They often crop up in fiction – Eeyore from *Winnie the Pooh*, or Marvin the Paranoid Android in the *Hitchhiker's Guide to the Galaxy*. Other people are just the opposite – always seeing good things in their life, exuding cheerfulness, and generally looking on the bright side of whatever happens. They are more like the fictional character Pollyanna – the little girl who was sunny and cheerful (sometimes too cheerful) in even the most unpromising situations.

How did people come to be so different? Perhaps they were born like that. Maybe happiness or unhappiness reflect inborn traits that stay with you throughout life? If so, we need to recognize that there will be elements of your happiness or otherwise that can't be changed, in your work and elsewhere – some feelings come from nature rather than nurture.

And research has shown that happiness does indeed in part depend on your genes. So your job feelings don't just come from the job; they also come from you. In this chapter we'll look at some findings about how different people are hard-wired to have different feelings. Studies have examined three topics: the consistency of happiness levels at different times, the extent to which this consistency is due to inheritance, and the happiness role of continuing personality features.

Once a happy person, always a happy person?

First, we know that everyone has ups and downs – a person's happiness level isn't always exactly the same. But there is a lot of within-person similarity from situation to situation. In studies carried out in many countries, people have been asked to complete questionnaires like the ones we've put in Chapter 3, doing that months or years apart. Think of the findings in terms of the rank-order of people's scores: number 1 is the most happy person, number 2 the next most happy, and so on to the least happy person in the sample. If happiness is pretty fixed, then the rank-order of individuals should be consistent whenever an individual takes the test: people high in the happiness league on one occasion should also be high in the league at another time. Does that work out?

Well not perfectly, if only because of what is technically called "measurement error" – unavoidable inaccuracies linked to technical factors. But the rank-order of individuals in a sample remains extremely similar between occasions. There's great consistency in people's happiness, so that those more happy on the first occasion are likely to be more happy next time. That holds good across global indicators like life satisfaction and (looking at negative feelings) general depression, and also for job satisfaction scores. Consistency of job well-being is especially strong for people who stay in the same job (for whom influences from the environment presumably remain similar), but it is only slightly less high for people who have changed their job; if you're satisfied with your present job, you'll probably be satisfied with your next one.

The consistency of happiness has also been shown in studies that track people between different kinds of situations. One approach is to ask the same people about their feelings at different times when they have moved into contrasting settings – for example during leisure activities and when at work. Sure enough, the happiness rank-order is substantially maintained: if you're happier than other people in some kinds of situations, you'll probably be happier than them elsewhere.

These facts make it clear that individuals have what is in effect their own "set-point" or baseline of happiness or unhappiness. Australian researchers Bruce Headey and Alexander Wearing have developed that idea into a "dynamic equilibrium model." This means that, although happiness does change because of things that happen to you (that's the "dynamic" bit), it later returns to your personal "equilibrium level." That process has been illustrated in a recent investigation into workers moving between jobs. Job satisfaction increased substantially after people started in a new position (that's the good news), but it returned towards their set-point levels in subsequent years (not so good news). This has also been found in studies recording people's feelings across a period of time after marriage or widowhood – sadly, the honeymoon effect isn't permanent, and neither (happily) is the grief experienced after loss of a partner.

So people have their own baseline level of happiness or unhappiness, and they are likely to revert to that level at some time after disruptions – whether those are positive or negative. Other research has asked whether these baselines are on average at the neutral point or whether individuals are in general relatively more happy than unhappy. From several kinds of study we can see that set-points are usually just slightly positive. For example, suppose a nationwide sample of people is asked to rate their happiness feelings from negative to positive. Their scores will be found to range quite widely, but the average is likely to be slightly above zero. On average, people look – just a little – on the bright side.

Learning from twins

But are these consistent personal baselines inherited? The answer is yes, partly. This gene effect has been shown in studies of the two members of twin pairs. Clearly not all pairs are the same: some twins are "identical," and others are "nonidentical." Identical twins are born from the same fertilized egg (they are "monozygotic"), and so they have an identical genetic structure. But nonidentical twins have come from two different eggs (they are "dizygotic") and have on average only one half of their genes in common. (End of basic biology lecture.)

This crucial difference makes it possible to learn about the impact of inheritance on many aspects of physical health and psychological features. We can do this by comparing the two kinds of twin in relation to the environments they have experienced. One kind of study looks at twins who have been brought up together (that is, in the same environment), and another type examines those who have been separated soon after birth and lived in different surroundings. The general idea is to see how similar or different they end up – depending on the circumstances of their upbringing and on whether twins are identical (with the same genes) or nonidentical (with partly different genes).

It all sounds straightforward but it isn't really, and researchers have their disagreements about details. For example, you need to consider whether twins that are identical in fact get treated in a more similar manner than their nonidentical counterparts. If that happens, identical twins have a more similar environment than those who are nonidentical, even though the two pairs in a study are defined as being brought up in the same kind of setting. Then again, how truly different are the environments of separated twins? They may move into family settings which appear contrasting but in practice remain similar in social and economic terms. Which statistical procedures should be used? And there are plenty more issues to debate.

Mercifully for us, there is a general consensus in the conclusion despite disagreements about the detail: people's level of happiness is without doubt partly inherited. That applies to global happiness about life in general and to feelings specifically about paid work, such as your job satisfaction. Job feelings are determined by your own inherited characteristics as well as by job features themselves. Some people have been dealt a deck of genes which makes them more likely to be happy than others.

It's not just happiness, of course. Research has shown genetic effects for many other psychological features – general intelligence and other cognitive abilities, traits of personality, specific preferences and attitudes, and broad outlooks like religious conservatism and racial prejudice. Those are all partly inherited; although your upbringing can certainly make a difference, a great deal of "you" has come from your genes.

You can better understand gene effects if you think about developments over a period of years. Inherited features lead people into very different kinds of situation (different schools, friendship networks, social settings, work roles, and so on), and those different situations have different effects on personal development, feelings and behavior. For instance, people inherit particular abilities which might give rise to certain sorts of education and jobs, and those different environments over time come to have their own impact on happiness. In that way, high-intelligence children learn more at school and may gain qualifications which allow them to move into more complex jobs than children with lower intelligence (which is partly inherited). The two kinds of job are linked to differences in job satisfaction (higher scores are found in more complex jobs), so that genetic effects on mental ability can indirectly over the years create differences in job happiness. Other research with twins has found that occupational level and even wages received are also in part inherited; your genes lead to patterns of behavior and skill acquisition which become reflected in your job success.

So we can be certain that happiness is moderately consistent across time and between situations (the chapter's first point), and also that this consistency has a strong genetic component (second). Everyone has a lot of room for change, and you can certainly make a difference to your own feelings. But there's a limit to what you can do to improve your happiness of a continuing kind – to an extent you are fixed as you are.

Applying these research conclusions to the Top Twelve job features in this book, it's clear that although those are certainly important they need to be understood in the context of inherited dispositions. Comparing the two happiness sources in a single study has shown that job content has a bigger well-being impact than personal characteristics:

feelings in a job are determined mainly by the nature of your job, but there's no getting away from the fact that your own characteristics also make a contribution.

Traits of personality

The third issue raised at the beginning of the chapter concerned personality. Linked to the idea of people's own "set-point" (above), perhaps there's such a thing as a happy or an unhappy personality – your feelings depend on your personality traits. That possibility has received lots of research attention, and a clear pattern is emerging.

Let's start by asking what psychologists mean by "personality." The popular idea might involve being a noticeable sort of individual, as in the popular reference to having a "big personality." Instead, we should think in terms of separate aspects or "dimensions" of personality – the ways in which people differ from each other in their consistent outlooks and preferences. For instance, a personality questionnaire may cover a large number of different styles (we'll look at some examples in a minute), with individuals describing their usual behavior and their likes or dislikes. These self-descriptions can then be analyzed to find the main groupings of specific items, the ones that occur together in the same person and can be said collectively to represent a trait or dimension of personality. (Sometimes, a study will ask *other* people who know the individual to describe him or her through the same questionnaire items.)

Personality researchers have identified a large number of traits of that kind, and with so many to choose from psychologists differ in the ones they emphasize. You can find examples at the web-site http://ipip.ori.org/ipip or particular questions at http://www.shldirect.com/. For instance, questionnaire scales shown in the first of those sites include traits of adaptability, cautiousness, dutifulness, exhibitionism, independence, orderliness, recklessness, sensitivity, and timidity. You can think of yourself and the people you know in those kinds of ways.

Traits themselves cluster together into groups, and it's currently popular to view those in terms of the "Big Five" "factors" of personality – sets of several similar characteristics that go together. The factors are usually named as Neuroticism, Extraversion, Openness to Experience, Agreeableness, and Conscientiousness. It's obviously an oversimplification to think of personality and differences between people in only five ways, but the Big Five do account for a lot of those differences.

The factors are described in the psychological literature like this:

- *Neuroticism* is usually taken to include continuing high levels of anxiety, depression, hostility and moodiness, with low Neuroticism scores sometimes labeled positively as "emotional stability." As with the other factors, there are wide differences between people; where do you fall in this respect?
- *Extraversion* can be thought of as two overlapping ways to "turn outward" (which is what "extraversion" means): a group of traits like sociability, friendliness, gregariousness and talkativeness (an "affiliative" tendency); and other traits like assertiveness, social potency, energy, optimism and influence on others (sometimes technically described as "surgency"). You can probably picture yourself in those terms.
- *Openness to Experience* covers "thinking" interests. The factor can be separated into either an artistic orientation (a sensitivity to aesthetic and cultural issues) or a more general intellectual emphasis on conceptual and abstract topics, but the two often go together. What about you?
- *Agreeableness* covers interpersonal features such as cooperativeness, modesty, trustworthiness, sympathy for others and consideration of people's wishes. This sounds good, but interestingly success in some pushful sales jobs has been found to require a *low* score on agreeableness. (It's pleasing to know that many other salespeople need to have *high* scores.)
- *Conscientiousness* is a tendency to act in two ways concerned with getting things done: first in terms of

achievement orientation, proactivity, striving, and a determination to attain goals; and second as dependability, planfulness, self-discipline, a concern for order, and an acceptance of routines and authority. Those two aspects usually but not always go together. For instance, some very determined and ambitious people aren't very reliable and dependable.

Researchers have examined those five aspects of personality in many countries. The usual approach is for individuals to complete questionnaire items which are known from lots of previous analyses to cover each of the factors. Some psychologists like to divide people into different categories or "types" separated with either a low score or a high score on a factor, for instance as either "introverts" or "extraverts." We often do that in everyday discussions, but in scientific analyses any cut-off point separating people into types suffers from being arbitrary – different researchers may define their "types" at different levels so they end up not comparing like with like.

Whether as dimensions or separated division into types, personality traits by definition remain part of you over a long period of time. Slight shifts have been found to occur through life, but generally a trait remains at much the same level across the years. On the other hand, happiness is linked directly to a present situation; it changes from time to time as a result of what happens in each particular setting. Ever-changing happiness doesn't sound like unchanging personality, does it?

But there is a strong connection. Despite the clear difference in time-focus between current happiness and a long-term trait, research has shown convincingly that some continuing personality features are quite closely related to short-term happiness feelings. Differences in feeling happy or unhappy in particular situations are linked to some of the Big Five personality factors.

The strongest connection is the one you would expect – a negative (reverse) association with the personality trait of Neuroticism. People who are consistently across situations more anxious and depressed (that is, with a more "neurotic" personality) are also less happy than others in a particular setting (and in the next one, and in the next one, and . . .). This continuing link has been shown both for global well-being (life satisfaction and similar measures) and also for job-related feelings of satisfaction and emotional exhaustion.

It comes about because a person's typical unhappiness (represented by the personality factor of Neuroticism) gets reflected in negative feelings during particular episodes: people who feel bad about things in general don't suddenly change their outlook when thinking about their job. So, when a worker describes his or her job satisfaction, there is a connection with his or her continuing level of Neuroticism. Whatever the actual content of a job, it's likely to be more disliked by those people who are generally more down-hearted than are others.

Other personality–happiness links are less obvious. Between-person differences in Extraversion are accompanied by similar rank-order differences in global happiness and well-being at work; a person who scores more highly on the continuing trait of Extraversion is also more likely to be happy – both in relation to his or her job and in life as a whole. There's something about having the characteristics of extraversion which leads to being more satisfied with your job and with your life in general.

Happiness levels also go along with the personality factors of Conscientiousness and Agreeableness (see the definitions above), although not as strongly. For instance, more achievement-oriented people (an aspect of Conscientiousness) are more satisfied with many aspects of their job. In general, if we know about a person's continuing traits, we can make a fairly good estimate of his or her level of happiness in a job relative to other job-holders.

These personality influences on happiness don't deny the importance of events around you. In Chapters 4 to 6 we established that the Top Twelve features of a job are crucially important for happiness or unhappiness; we can now add the fact that those environmental influences are felt through the filter of people's personalities. Feelings come from a combination of both.

It's a complex picture, of course, since any level of happiness involves genetic influences, personality-related behaviors and also the environment itself. Let's look at each step in the process.

First, people's baseline for happiness is largely inherited, and so is their level of, say, Extraversion. Those two go together, so that Extraverts are to some degree born with a propensity to higher levels of happiness than are Introverts. However, there's more to it than that. Inherited Extraversion also promotes happiness through some styles of daily living. For instance, extraverted individuals are more likely to seek out the company of other people and be drawn to jobs that involve social interaction. Given that social contact is (up to a point) associated with more happiness (see Chapters 4 and 5), extraverts can become more happy because they place themselves in more social situations. There is also the fact that they may enjoy social activities which introverts find boring, so that identical social contacts can have different impacts on the two kinds of personality.

The causal process also works in the opposite direction. Being friendly with other people is likely to bring about pleasing reactions from them, as they respond in kind – similarly helping you, or otherwise providing good companionship in ways which in turn make you feel more happy. It's unfair, but extraverts have the advantage here.

Personality-related differences in happiness thus build up over a long time, as lifestyles come to differ because of your particular traits. Individuals with more Neuroticism or Extraversion behave in different ways from people with lower scores on those traits, and the different nature of their daily activities can bring about less or more happiness respectively. In turn, the experience of enjoying or disliking extraverted activity (for example) can reinforce the associated disposition, so these personality-and-happiness differences can become established over a lifetime.

However, it's not just a question of trait-related differences in what people do; there are also differences in styles of thinking. For example, people with personalities that are more Neurotic typically look out for worrying possibilities, more often seeing threats and possible dangers in the environment. With those mental emphases, more Neurotic individuals are more likely to think of reasons to be unhappy; they'll expect a measure of unhappiness as their default position – and sure enough this expectation gets fulfilled.

As another example, extraverted people (shown above to be more happy on average than introverts) often think differently from those who are introverted. For instance, extraverts have been found to make more "downward" social comparisons (see Self-question 1 in the next chapter, page 123) – noticing more frequently than introverts when other people's situations are worse than their own. As Chapter 8 will describe, mental comparisons of that "downward" kind are generally likely to aid happiness, whereas "upward" comparisons (against those who are better positioned than you) can encourage gloom.

In addition, extraverts tend less often to dwell on the downside of a situation, and are more likely to do things without reflecting about possible consequences. Extraverts thus generally spend less time thinking about possible unpleasant happenings, they more often just get on with it; and they are on average more happy. This isn't necessarily a good thing every time – their limited reflection can of course lead to unwise risk-taking and thus an unhappy outcome.

These personality-related differences in styles of behavior and thinking are important in another respect. They point to ways in which people might be able to increase their happiness. If you could identify your actions and thoughts that are consistently linked to unhappiness, perhaps you could try to change those. We'll look at that in Chapter 10 when we'll describe some steps that can be taken to increase happiness, particularly at work. First however let's look at thinking styles a little more closely – the ways you typically reflect on and make sense of your situation. The next chapter introduces seven questions you can ask yourself which bear directly on your likelihood of feeling bad or feeling good.

Come to think about it
. . . happiness is relative

The English poet William Cowper had the right idea when he wrote in 1782:

Happiness depends, as Nature shows,
Less on exterior things than most suppose.

We've seen that happiness at work (or anywhere else) depends on "exterior things" in an environment (Chapters 4 to 6) and also on "interior things" like personal baselines and traits of personality (Chapter 7). It's now time to turn to the impact of subjective reactions and mental processes. Happiness isn't just a direct response to an external event, like an electric light that has been switched on. Instead, the way we interpret something can strongly affect our feelings about it – more like an electric light that can make itself brighter or dimmer.

Nobody is affected in a completely passive way by the world around them. Everyone looks at what happens through filters of their own memories and expectations. These interpretations can be conscious and detailed in terms of careful reflection, or they can be quick and unnoticed in immediate thoughts. What they share in common is that they influence how "exterior things" are experienced. And the important point for this chapter is that we all have different memories, ideas and expectations. In everyday terms, some people looking at a half-empty glass see it as almost full, others see it as more nearly empty.

So our happiness level is not completely fixed by what happens to us; it comes also from our own thoughts. Some people take this idea to extremes. There are self-help books out there that will tell you you're the architect of everything that happens to you, and that you can change your life by thinking about it in a certain way. In effect, they say "it's all in the mind." That's an exaggerated view, but like many such views it's partly correct – "a lot of it" is in the mind. And maybe there are things you can do to "change your mind." We'll look at those in Chapters 9 and 10.

Happiness is based on key environmental features and on your personal baseline and traits – we've already discussed those – but it's also linked to your comparisons and thoughts about:

- what other people have got
- what else might have happened
- what you expected
- how effective you've been
- your direction of progress
- what you are used to
- how important something is to you.

Let's look at each of those in turn.

Seven sorts of thought

The box opposite gives a set of seven ways of thinking you probably use every week. They make up a sort of internal framework of how happy you are. Although you usually don't notice their impact, they help to explain why a given level of a job feature can have different effects on happiness or unhappiness for different people. The "external things" may be fixed, but you can think about them in different ways.

Let's look at these in turn, reviewing some of the issues that affect your answers to the questions in the right-hand column.

Happiness-affecting thoughts	Questions you might ask yourself
1. Comparisons with other people	*"Are others better-off or worse-off?"*
2. Comparisons with alternative situations	*"How else could things have turned out?"*
3. Comparisons with what you expected	*"Has this turned out as I thought it would?"*
4. Assessments of your own effectiveness	*"Am I handling this well?"*
5. Mental comparisons with a desirable trend	*"How are things going? Getting better, worse, or about the same?"*
6. Assessments of novelty or familiarity	*"Is the situation unusual or is it familiar?"*
7. Attractiveness ratings of a job feature	*"How personally important are these bits of my job?"*

Self-question 1. Are others better-off or worse-off?

For English writer Thomas Shadwell (1642–1692), "no man is happy except by comparison."[1] That's certainly overdoing it, but the general idea is right. Research into what are called "social comparison processes" has shown that feelings of happiness or unhappiness are often affected by a person's thoughts about other people. (It's the "other people" bit that makes the comparisons "social.") Your own reaction to an event or situation is often influenced by how you view the position of others.

If you compare yourself against very fortunate people, you'll often become less happy than if you focus on people who are worse-off than yourself, not only in financial terms but of course those too. Even though your situation (an "external thing" in the terms above) remains the same, your feelings of happiness or unhappiness can vary depending on which kind of comparison you make. Your grandparents probably told you that "worse things happen at sea," or that there's always someone in a worse position than you. Unconsciously (we presume) they were applying this research.

Putting yourself in mental context against other people in this way is usually described as either an "upward" or a "downward" comparison. An "upward" mental comparison is with someone whose situation is better than your own, and "downward" comparisons are with people in a worse position. As a rule, comparing yourself with someone better-off is a good way of upsetting yourself, and comparative thoughts that are downward (about those who are worse-off) are often beneficial.

Here are some examples. If your office is reasonably comfortable you may be satisfied, until you learn that people in another company have new and luxurious conditions. On the other hand, if your office is reasonably comfortable but others are working in really grotty surroundings, you may well be satisfied.

A friend of ours who was unemployed for a long period became used to comparing his situation to that of other jobless people, and found he came to terms with that. However, when he was short-listed for a highly-paid position, his outlook suddenly changed. Once again he looked at himself against a wealthy and busy "reference group" (a bit of psychological jargon there) and soon felt dissatisfied with what he had and could do. Similar comparison effects can be seen more generally among employed people in 2009: some of those didn't much like their job in 2007, but in a time of economic gloom they more appreciated what they had in relation to other less fortunate people.

Comparisons of that kind are being made all the time, and research comparing unhappy versus happy individuals has shown that unhappiness goes along with more comparisons of the upward kind; unhappy people are more likely to look out for better-off others and feel bad when they find them. Some people jealously watch "celebrities" for their beauty and glitzy lifestyle; that's a good way to become dissatisfied with their own situation, not to mention their body-image. On the other hand, individuals who are more happy generally pay less attention to other people's position in relation to their own – they make fewer "social comparisons."

Some research has checked out these ideas in relation to satisfaction with pay. Quite obviously, this comparison process has a big impact. The actual amount that you receive is of course important, but so too are your thoughts about other people's pay and the norms in your business. If you're earning more than similar other people, that's great. For you anyway. However, if you hear something – through newspaper articles, your colleagues' complaints, or your union's wage claim – that suggests you're underpaid in relation to other people doing similar or (using whatever definition) lesser work, you are more likely to be dissatisfied with what you get. Your level of pay doesn't change, but your feelings about it do.

Comparisons of that kind also spill over into how satisfied you are with the other features of your job. We've mentioned working conditions already, but others in the Top Twelve list are also judged in this way. Good or bad feelings don't come merely from your job's features themselves (unless those are really extreme); they can also depend on how you interpret your situation in relation to that of other people.

Self-question 2. How else could things have turned out?

A similar kind of thought is about situations that might instead have occurred. (These are technically described as "counterfactual" situations – contrary to the facts.) "Upward" comparisons in this case are against possible outcomes that would have been better for you (but which didn't happen), and "downward" comparisons are against alternative situations which could have been worse. Those two kinds of thoughts have opposite effects on your feelings: upward comparisons are discouraging and maybe upsetting, whereas noticing possible unpleasant alternatives (through downward contrary-to-the-fact comparisons) can often be comforting – perhaps things aren't so bad after all.

That contrast was illustrated in a recent study of Olympic medalists. Winning competitors who received silver medals for attaining second place were on average found to be less happy with their position than were bronze medalists, the ones who only managed third place. Many of the second-place winners appeared to base their feelings in part on counterfactual comparisons that were upward, thinking "I could have won," "I missed this by a split second" or something like that. On the other hand, athletes in third place were more likely to make downward comparisons, being pleased to have reached the medal positions ("I did better than all the rest"). In the Beijing 2008 Olympics, the British women's rowing team were distraught at getting the silver medal; their expectations, aspirations and wants conspired to make what would otherwise have been a highly respectable result seem disastrous to them.

Sticking with the Beijing Olympics a moment, it's instructive to look at how results were reported internationally. The British team overall thought they might come sixth or seventh in the table of gold medals. When they came fourth in this table, their automatic downward comparison (against an alternative outcome that wasn't as good) led them to feel elated. The USA came third on the gold-medal criterion, but American reporting – in which the tables were based not on gold medals but on the total medals regardless of order – put them first. In that way, Americans' counterfactual comparisons could only be downward, reinforcing their pleasure at the outcome.

Another effect of might-have-been thoughts has been investigated in terms of "post-decision rationalization" – the way people deliberate after a decision which they can't change. One research study looked at students' thoughts about colleges which had either rejected or accepted their application for admission. Students who were more happy than others had come to view the colleges that had turned them down as less attractive than before and the ones which accepted them as even more attractive. In other words, they changed their views in response to negative decisions which had not turned out as hoped – a process of rationalization. On the other hand, students who continued to strongly value the colleges that had rejected them were significantly more unhappy. They still emphasized the high desirability of something which had not happened – an upward counterfactual comparison.

In job settings, counterfactual comparisons of these upward or downward kinds can affect reactions to any feature. It's not just the level of that feature that makes you happy or unhappy; it's also how you focus on possible alternatives – the might-have-beens. This is where you can often take control; you can't change how things are but you can dwell less on not winning a prize every time. We'll see in Chapter 10 how turning your mind away from negative possibilities might sometimes increase happiness at work, or indeed in any other context.

Self-question 3. Has this turned out as I thought it would?

A third way in which people's mental interpretation of a situation affects their happiness is in terms of expectation. It's clear from daily experience that a positive event which was a surprise to you can be even more pleasant than one which you had been expecting. (Ingrained in Western culture is the Biblical story of the Prodigal Son. You may remember that his father was mightily pleased when the Prodigal came back against all expectation, while he took his "good" son's average conduct as read.) Conversely, a negative event which was foreseen can have a less strong impact than one which was a complete surprise. It can still be nasty, but perhaps not as nasty as it would have been if it came out of the blue.

This can happen in the workplace too. When you change your situation, you usually have some ideas about what will happen in your new position. If those expectations are not met, you are likely to feel even more discouraged than you would otherwise have been.

Unhappiness of that kind is partly of your own making, because you have set some expectations too high. If you think you will meet the very difficult targets you've set yourself (to be extremely successful in a task or to get a lot of work finished by tonight), you may be asking for trouble, especially if you're already loaded with other problems. Yes, you need to have positive expectations about how well you can do (that's part of "self-confidence"), but don't expect too much or you'll feel bad about your inevitable failures. Such a tendency is part of a general style of "perfectionism" – setting standards for yourself that are invariably very high. You may be one of those people who need to keep checking their perfectionism in the same way as they check their blood pressure; take a look, so you can keep both down to reasonable levels. The general point is that your reactions to your own performance of course depend on how well you've done, but they also come from what you expected.

This third happiness-affecting thought is sometimes used to their advantage by negotiators, politicians and others, in terms of "managing expectations." For example, if some future desirable event is repeatedly "talked down" as very unlikely, even a small positive movement can make people feel better because they weren't expecting much. Or a company's prediction of poor financial results can lead investors to feel better if they later find that results aren't so bad after all.

So the happiness or unhappiness associated with a certain level of a job feature isn't fixed – it can depend on what you expected. Expectations come partly from your own experience and personal styles of thinking, but also from the views of other people with whom you've discussed what might happen. So we mustn't forget that perspectives and interpretations can be shaped by people around you, who can lead you to certain kinds of expectation (and to other thoughts described in this chapter).

So if your colleagues repeatedly grumble about how bad they feel doing this job and point out other people who have something better, your job satisfaction will almost certainly suffer. Or if a spouse or partner draws your attention to upward social comparisons (yes we *are* talking about "keeping up with the Joneses") or more attractive possibilities of the might-have-been kind, you can easily come to feel more negatively about your situation. (If the suggestions are repeated many times – some call it "nagging" – feelings about the spouse/partner can go downhill as well.)

Self-question 4. Am I handling this well?

Many situations are brought about partly by your own decisions and actions, and feelings about those situations can depend in part on how successful you think you have been. Perhaps something bad happened partly because of your mistakes. That can make you even more despondent as you blame yourself. And a good result is even more pleasing if you were at least partly responsible, because you feel satisfied with yourself as well as about the event itself.

This process applies generally. In thousands of small ways your thoughts about your own effectiveness can modify the happiness or unhappiness that comes from your job. Feeling good about how you're handling things can help you feel better about your job more generally. Once again, the way you think about features and events is important for your feelings, over and above what actually happens.

Self-question 5. How are things going? Getting better, worse, or about the same?

In some jobs you are stuck with job features (the chance to use skill, social contact, and so on) whose level hasn't shifted for ages. But there are other jobs where things keep changing. We know from research studies that features that are improving or deteriorating can have a positive or negative impact which is different from the impact of that same feature when it remains constant. People – in jobs and elsewhere – often react more to changes in their situation than to conditions that remain stable.

Often without thinking about it, we recognize trends – like whether our task activity is moving forward or not – and our thoughts about the magnitude and direction of change can alter how pleased or unhappy we are with a situation. If you perceive that things are getting better you are likely to feel more positive about them than if they had been like that for ages. You're happy with the improvement and you infer that it may get better still. And a situation you see as deteriorating is similarly viewed as more unpleasant than others which are like that situation but not getting worse.

Over and above the direct impact of an event or situation (an "external thing" in the chapter's opening quotation), awareness of positive change can thus make us optimistic and cheerful. On the other hand, a perceived trend in the opposite direction often yields pessimism and unhappiness as it starts to color our expectations of the future.

You've probably noticed that predicted trends of that kind can become "self-fulfilling prophecies." For instance, movement of the stock market can be influenced in that way, as gloom about an outlook becomes magnified by fashion to make future share movements even more negative. Press coverage of the credit crunch in 2008/9 centered around job losses and bad news, and paid very little heed to those companies adding jobs to their roster. How much less insecure people would have felt if newspaper headlines had covered job creation as fully as company problems. The economic slowdown may perhaps have been softened a little if expectations had lifted and people felt more confident moving their money around.

The general idea is pretty straightforward, but we want to stress the point. Don't only think of happiness or unhappiness as arising from a current situation as it stands; think also about how that situation has changed and is changing. As concluded in other sections, the same situation does not invariably lead to a certain level of happiness; its impact is partly determined by how you interpret it.

Self-question 6. Is the situation unusual or familiar?

Psychologists and physiologists have explored many aspects of what is usually referred to as "adaptation." Colloquially you might call it "acclimatization" even though there's no literal change in climate involved. Events and circumstances that are repeated or remain unchanged over a period of time come to have a diminishing impact on us –

physiologically as well as psychologically. For instance, hot water comes to seem less hot (or sea water becomes less cold when you go for a swim), and a mild smell becomes unnoticed over time. Similarly, we may gradually feel less strongly about other people and events, becoming more tolerant of a negative aspect of life or finding ourselves less attracted to a positive feature.

This process of adaptation over time has been studied in individuals who suffer an accident leading to disability or become seriously ill, documenting how people gradually become less unhappy as they adjust to their situation. They discover thoughts and actions – not necessarily on purpose – that help them to cope better with their bad situation. Similarly, unpleasant or stressful jobs can become less troublesome after a time. A camp-ground worker who has to clean out public toilets (in the USA referred to as restrooms) illustrates the process: "There's some bad odors sometimes – and some messes. But you get used to it. I don't really mind anymore."[2]

On the positive side, job features you enjoy can gradually become less rewarding. They may start as new and exciting but later become "OK but a bit boring." (We've been told that husbands can be like that.) The "hedonic treadmill" comes in here. ("Hedonic" means "related to pleasure.") You can work (in the "treadmill" of life) to reach a certain level of satisfaction, but your achievement gradually becomes less pleasing to you, so you have to keep working to reach the same level of satisfaction again. This process is sometimes illustrated in terms of income: people seek more money, but then their increased income becomes customary and familiar for them, and they next have to seek even more money if they are to be satisfied in those terms again.

Does that mean that it's pointless to seek higher income to make you happy? Not at all! A central theme of this book is that happiness comes from a variety of different features and also from several processes which affect your thinking about those features. No single feature can make you happy on its own, but any one of them can be particularly important to you at any time. Having money is generally desirable and particularly so when you're broke (see Chapters 4 and 5), but there's a lot more to happiness than being wealthy.

The opposite of adaptation is when a situation contrasts strongly with the usual one. By and large, it is deviations from what we are used to which have the greatest impact on us. For example, the first reaction in visiting a new country can be quite intense – the language, the food, the architecture are starkly different from what you are used to. In the area of this book, contrast effects have been studied in terms of hassles occurring on successive days. Having to cope with a lot of minor problems is in any case unpleasant and possibly distressing, but people have been found to feel relatively better after a contrast with something that was even worse – when the previous day was really, really bad. The switch from a very negative input to one that is nasty but less negative than before makes you feel less bad than you otherwise would have been.

The reverse contrast is also important. When your situation changes from good to bad, you are likely to feel even worse than you would have done without the shift. This has been shown for mothers juggling with the demands of both work and home. If a previous day had been relatively easy in terms of work–home conflict, having to juggle the two kinds of activity on the next day was particularly upsetting. A sharp negative contrast with earlier easy conditions makes a day's stressors particularly painful.

The effects of contrast and adaptation are also shown in research into people moving between jobs. Generally job satisfaction increases as you move into a new job – through contrast with the old one and because the new position has features that you like. However, as time passes and you've had repeated experience of the new surroundings and activities, satisfaction has been found to decline through a typical process of adaptation. At the same time, other externals can kick in and undo some of the good the change did in the first place. Familiarity does not necessarily breed contempt but it does reduce something's attractiveness.

We come down to individual interpretations again: a particular feature does not have a standard impact on happiness or unhappiness – it depends on how it fits with your experience and thoughts.

Self-question 7. How personally important are these bits of my job?

Your reaction to job features like those in Chapters 5 and 6 is particularly affected by how strongly you value them. We know that (for example) variety ("vitamin" 4) or social contact (6) at work are important for job happiness, but also that people differ in the degree to which they want to have those features – for some workers they matter a lot, but others aren't so much bothered whether they are present or absent. These between-person differences in the salience or otherwise of a job feature have been shown to make a difference to its impact on job happiness.

Job happiness or unhappiness are more strongly linked to a particular feature if that feature is judged to be personally important. For instance, the job satisfaction of people who are keen to work in a team is much influenced by whether or not their job involves team-working, but that's not the case for people who aren't concerned about team-working or its absence. Put simply, a job feature greatly affects your feelings at work only if it's something that matters to you – because of the kind of person you are (for instance, your extraverted personality means you want social contact) or because you particularly seek that feature at the moment (you're broke and seriously need money). For someone else, who isn't concerned whether the feature is absent or present, quite different aspects of the job can be the ones that make the difference.

Once again, job features aren't the only cause of your feelings at work. Sure, your job happiness or unhappiness comes largely from the content of that job, but it also depends on you – in this case your preferences and wants in relation to what you've got.

Self-questions: Overview

The account of research findings in this chapter helps to explain why the job features in earlier chapters don't have a standard impact. The characteristics reviewed there are certainly the most important ones for happiness or unhappiness in a job (the "exterior things" in the chapter's opening quotation), but they don't have the same effect on everyone. Their impact is shaped by happiness baselines and personality traits (in Chapter 7), and also by the seven kinds of thought identified in the present chapter – the personal benchmarks we've been reviewing. That's why we described happiness as "relative" in the title of this chapter; it's not only affected by the conditions and events in your life, it's relative to the way you look at those.

The seven thoughts have been talked about one at a time, but of course, several of them can come into play at once. Of the seven, the last one – the operation of personal salience – has a particular impact. Job features make you feel pleased or unhappy in proportion to their salience to you: how much they are personally important or how much you want them to be present. This means that the Top Twelve features in your job need to be viewed in relation to your feelings about them – how personally important is each one?

What do you look for in a job?

People's different wants, for job content as well as for other things, have been studied in terms of "values." A value concerns what a person consistently approves of, prefers against alternatives, wants, or considers important.

Values are central to everyone's style of living. They operate as broad social or cultural norms in countries and organizations as a whole, and also as individual people's preferences and dislikes guiding everyday activity. Values range in scope from approval or disapproval of broad religious principles or political ideologies to minor preferences such as about which program to watch on television. Sometimes values have a moral or ethical basis, concerned with what is right or wrong, but they also concern (as emphasized here) whatever is desirable or undesirable for you personally – your evaluations of features in the world. (Moral themes might of course play a part in those evaluations.)

It's clear that different people have very different personal values of these kinds – they favor different activities and viewpoints. Think about the many kinds of hobbies that appeal to some individuals and horrify others – stamp-collecting, sky-diving, bird-watching, soccer-supporting, opera-loving, table-tennis playing, gardening, and so on. None of these are objectionable as such, but some people are horrified by the idea of spending time in that way. They just don't understand how anyone can find (say) sticking stamps in an album to be remotely interesting. Now think about work – the many kinds of job activities that are either liked or disliked by different people: repairing cars, cutting into flesh, risking huge sums of money, caring for people near death, melting steel, being a prison guard, scanning items in a supermarket, analyzing financial accounts, fighting wars, checking railway tickets, and so on. The spread of people's preferences is huge; in some cases there truly is "no accounting for taste."

Let's focus on some personal values that concern work – preferences for aspects of a job. Which aspects of your work particularly matter to you, and which ones aren't of great concern? It's important to know about these different personal priorities, since (as shown above) job satisfaction and other forms of well-being arise from the features that you more strongly value rather than from others which are of little concern to you. And your values define the kind of job which might make you happy; if your work doesn't fit your values, you're in trouble.

Remember that we're talking here about evaluations of any kind, not merely those with an ethical basis. Work values of that general kind have been studied in many ways, for example asking about average patterns in particular groups of people – such as men and women. There are of course differences between individual men and individual women, but on average the two sexes are found to have many similar preferences for job features. However, some job-feature values are markedly different. On average, women workers have been shown to place much greater emphasis than do men on pleasant social contacts, the chance to meet people, and emotional support from their colleagues. They also more strongly look for convenient working hours, whereas on average men will value good pay and the opportunity to use their initiative. Whether that's because they tend to have the option, even now, to leave child-care to the female partner is an unanswered question.

What about you? Questionnaire 4 on pages 138–139 covers the 12 key factors identified in Chapters 4 to 6. We asked you earlier to think about the presence or absence of those features in your present job, and now we suggest that instead you think about your *ideal* job: which job features would you like to have in a job that is perfect for you?

As in other cases, to avoid spoiling the page you might take a photocopy or simply jot down the numbers of your responses on a separate piece of paper. Or use the website as indicated on page 138

Your answers will probably be towards the right-hand side of the questionnaire, because all these job features were selected as being important on average for workers as a whole. However, it's good to try to spread out your responses between the features. That is because the goal is to identify which aspects you are not very concerned about as well as indicating the ones which are most important for you.

You might also like to think in more depth about certain of the job features, in terms of more specific aspects of the Top Twelve described earlier. For example, the sixth feature (Social Contacts) includes separately both the quantity and the quality of interactions (6a and 6b in the earlier list). And we've often spoken with women who are particularly concerned to have convenient working hours – one specific aspect within feature 3. Are there some particular components of an overall feature which you value especially highly, more than the other aspects of that feature? (If you're not sure what these components are, take a look at the table at the beginning of Chapter 5, page 72.)

By pausing to reflect in these ways you'll be able to build up a description of what really matters to you in a job and which features are of lower personal concern. Putting together questionnaire responses about your present job (what you've got – Questionnaire 3 on pages 106–107) and the features you really value (what you want – Questionnaire 4 on the next pages), you can next concentrate on those features which are not right for you – the ones with the wrong mix of "got" and "want." Those are the features where you scored either "too little" or "too much" on the first questionnaire and also particularly valued on the questionnaire in this chapter.

But what can you do with this information when you've gathered it all together? Is there anything you can change to bump up the troublesome features? There are no simple ways to make yourself happy in a job, but there are several steps you can consider taking. Those are suggested in the next two chapters.

Notes

1 In *The virtuoso*, published in 1676.

2 See page 202 of J. Bowe, M. Bowe and S. Streeter (eds.), *Gig: Americans talk about their work* (New York: Three Rivers Press, 2000).

Questionnaire 4: What matters to you in a job?
(A printable version of this questionnaire is available at www.psypress.com/joyofwork)

Thinking of your ideal job, the one that you'd really like, how important to you is the presence of each of these 12 features? Place a circle around the appropriate number in each case below.

		In my ideal job, presence of the feature is:					
		Not at all important	Slightly important	Moderately important	Very important	Extremely important	Essential
1	Personal influence (What you can change)	1	2	3	4	5	6
2	Using your abilities (Applying your strengths)	1	2	3	4	5	6
3	Demands and goals (What you have to do)	1	2	3	4	5	6
4	Variety (Different activities)	1	2	3	4	5	6
5	Clear requirements and outlook (Not too much uncertainty)	1	2	3	4	5	6
6	Social contacts (Enough and good dealings with others)	1	2	3	4	5	6

		Not at all important	Slightly important	Moderately important	Very important	Extremely important	Essential
			In my ideal job, presence of the feature is:				
7	Money (Getting paid well)	1	2	3	4	5	6
8	Adequate physical setting (Working conditions)	1	2	3	4	5	6
9	A valued role (Social consequences and self-worth)	1	2	3	4	5	6
10	Supportive supervision (Helpful in getting the job done)	1	2	3	4	5	6
11	Good career outlook (Security and prospects)	1	2	3	4	5	6
12	Fair treatment (For employees and others)	1	2	3	4	5	6

Today's date:

Actions as well as words

You might be wondering what you can do with all this information about research and theory. After all, maybe it's true that "actions speak louder than words."

Applied psychologists have their own take on that – "there's nothing as practical as a good theory." In other words you've got to understand what's going on under the bonnet before tinkering around with the engine. That's our belief. We hope readers have learned something about themselves and their situation. And we know that some will decide to leave things as they are. That's fine. However, others may want to make some changes. This chapter and the next one look at some possibilities.

First a word of warning: don't expect miracles. OK, that's three words of warning. Your current experience of life is the result of many thousands of events and decisions across many years; you can't turn those around overnight. Also, never mind that some self-help books have promised to change everything for you and transform your life. (Such books have sometimes been said to "overpromise and underdeliver." There are less polite ways of putting it.) Every book has its limitations when it comes to getting things done, but another proverb points out that "great oaks from little acorns grow." You certainly can aim for a succession of possibly small improvements.

Influences on happiness or unhappiness come from several different directions and combine in different ways for different people. One person's unhappiness at work may be mainly due to job content (rotten pay, overload, a bullying boss . . .), whereas someone else's can be more a question of personality. So we're not going to make "one size fits all" suggestions about how to become happier. Recommendations need to be tailored to different individuals.

Longer-term and short-term happiness

Research and common sense show that even generally happy individuals have times when they are anything but happy – they feel anxious about problems facing them or depressed because something has gone wrong. That applies in any area of life. People become worried about their amateur dramatic performance, fed-up with their partner or irritated by their children, in the same way that they sometimes dislike their jobs. As described in Chapter 3, it's usual – even healthy – to have mixed feelings about a situation or job, either because you feel differently about its different aspects or because your enjoyment varies from time to time. So you can be unhappy about your job at the present moment for all sorts of reasons, but you can still overall be positive about it. Short-term unhappiness in a job is part of life.

This raises the issue of how you feel long- and medium-term. Whether you're feeling at the moment miserable, euphoric or somewhere in between, how do you decide *overall* how happy you are? You can't afford to be swayed too much by a temporary good or bad mood. You must think in general, over several weeks or months. When we ask you in this chapter to think about your job and your feelings, try to look beyond the immediate present.

Nine steps towards job happiness

Here we go, then – some practical stuff. We've taken themes from the previous chapters and combined them with additional research into several different topics – people's career choice, the restructuring of jobs, clinical treatments, and self-help procedures of a general kind – to suggest ways in which you might think of improving your job situation. We've divided suggestions into nine different steps, but of course none of those happen in isolation – there's huge overlap.

Let's think in terms of three principal stages. First you review your feelings and your job situation (that's in Steps 1 to 4). Next consider your view of the world and how that affects the way you feel (Steps 5 to 7). Those two stages summarize your job and yourself. They'll be enough for one chapter. We'll leave the third stage to Chapter 10, looking there at what might be done both to improve a job (Step 8) and to change your personal styles of thinking (Step 9).

Many people, the authors of this volume included, get irritated by long lists of actions dictated by so-called experts. And working through these nine steps might seem a bit mechanical and tedious. So we want to emphasize that a "pick and mix" approach is fine if you prefer: have a quick look at what's on offer, and only try a few of the "goodies." If that partial approach seems helpful, you might like to think about the sequence as a whole another time.

First, review your job situation

Where does your job fit into our framework? Previous chapters have examined three key areas: your level of happiness, the characteristics of your job, and your main work values. Let's now look particularly at you and your own job situation in those three ways.

Step 1: Look at your job feelings

The book has emphasized that there are many kinds of happiness and unhappiness. Here we are interested specifically in your *job-related* well-being, rather than global happiness about life in general. Job feelings can be summarized by the two questionnaires presented in Chapter 3 – about your job satisfaction and about happy and unhappy feelings.

Have another look at Questionnaire 1: *Overall job satisfaction* (on pages 30–31). This covers 15 aspects of your job: how satisfied are you with those? If your overall average score is below about 4.50, you're less satisfied than the average worker. An average score of about 5.00 ("I'm moderately satisfied") is obviously better, but still less than many people might want. So, if you score less than about 5.00 on Overall Job Satisfaction, you need to think hard.

Before we move on, you might like to make a mental note of those job aspects which most cause dissatisfaction, and also the ones which scored the highest. Remember it's usual to have mixed feelings. Many people expect to live with some negative aspects in their world because those are outweighed by positive themes; that balancing process applies in a job as well as elsewhere.

The second questionnaire concerned *Feelings at work* (page 39). Maybe you've already worked out your average scores for positive (happy) and negative (unhappy) feelings. If not, try doing it now. Possible answers range like this:

Response number	Positive job feelings	Negative job feelings
1	Not at all happy	Not at all unhappy
2	Just a little happy	Just a little unhappy
3	Quite happy	Quite unhappy
4	Very happy	Very unhappy
5	Extremely happy	Extremely unhappy

How are your job feelings of those kinds? If your average positive score is less than 4 ("very happy") or your average negative feelings are more than 2 ("just a little unhappy"), things could clearly be better.

There are two main ways in which you can feel bad. The questionnaire's negative feelings include anxiety, tension and worry (items 3, 7 and 11), but it also contains gloomy, depressed and miserable (4, 8 and 12). Those two sets of items separately cover the two left-hand sections of the Happiness Wheel in Chapter 3: anxiety and depression respectively. Here it is again:

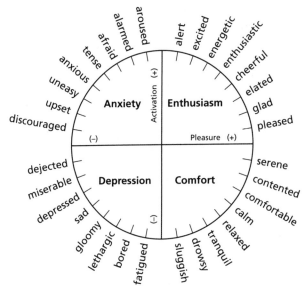

The Happiness Wheel

Is your job unhappiness more a question of anxiety or depression (recognizing that the two often go together)? As we said in Chapter 3, different kinds of positive or negative feelings are likely to occur when you're doing different kinds of things. The anxious kind of unhappiness (in the top-left section) usually comes from high demands and overload, whereas depression (bottom left) comes more from underload, failure to get where you want to be, or sheer boredom.

There are also differences on the right-hand side of the Happiness Wheel. Positive feelings may be a question of being enthusiastic, excited and interested (items 1, 5 and 9 in Questionnaire 2; the top-right section of the Wheel) or consist mainly of being contented, comfortable and relaxed (2, 6 and 10). Either of those kinds of feeling is nice, but both together are even better. The best kind of job puts you mainly in the top-right section (enthusiastic, excited and interested) with feelings from time to time in the bottom right of less activated happiness (contented, comfortable and relaxed). But don't forget that some negative feelings are unavoidable as you tackle difficult issues. Don't forget also that a bit of anxiety can be exactly what you need to kick-start your adrenalin. Think of the ace salesperson who's worried that his or her bonus payments may not be enough to pay the mortgage.

So, in seeking job happiness you should be looking for the sort of "feelings cocktail" that works for you. And keep in mind that even fairly happy people have a mix of feelings, some of which can be quite negative – we don't live in a world of incessant bliss. Nevertheless, if you are very widely dissatisfied for a lot of the time and have many unhappy reactions, then there's clearly a need for change.

Step 2: Look at your job

Assuming that your job feelings (at Step 1) were more negative than you'd like, you now have to ask why. That takes us first to Questionnaire 3 on pages 106–107: *Features in your job.*

That questionnaire covered the Top Twelve job characteristics – the ones which most influence happiness or unhappiness at work. Here it is again as Questionnaire 5 (on pages 148–149), but we've fiddled with it a bit by shading some of the columns. The shaded areas can be viewed as danger zones: if you score in such a zone, your job well-being is probably less than it should be.

If you haven't already filled in that questionnaire, now is a good time. Again, remember you should think about the past few weeks as a whole, not just today or some other brief period. You're after a rounded picture over a period of time.

If you rate any of the features as "very much too low" or "much too low" (with a score of 1 or 2), then you need to have a think about what to do about it. And ratings for the first six features (the "vitamins" which are "toxic" at high levels) that are either 6 or 7 ("much too high" or "very much too high") also suggest that something needs to change.

Chapters 5 and 6 also described specific subcomponents of some of the Top Twelve characteristics. For example,

feature 3 (Demands and Goals) involves the specific requirements caused by work–home conflict as well as other kinds
of demand, and Social Contacts (feature 6) might be thought
about separately in respect of quantity and quality or in
terms of interactions with colleagues and with clients. Are
any subcomponents particularly troubling you? Look out for
any that fall in the shaded danger zones.

How does your profile of job features look? Are there
some that may need attention? Which are they? How
extreme are your ratings – in some cases "much too" low or
high (scoring 1 or 7)? Again, try zeroing in on specific subcomponents. Are they sometimes the problem, rather than
the broader features listed in the questionnaire?

Step 3: Decide what you most want

Although the Top Twelve job characteristics are crucial for
people in general, Chapter 8 introduced the idea that individuals differ in their work values – their preferences for
certain features and activities more than others. It's very
likely that certain of the 12 job features are more important
to you than others.

Questionnaire 4 on pages 138–139 (headed *What
matters to you in a job?*) covered work values of those
kinds. If you didn't complete that at the time, have a go at it
now. As with Questionnaire 5, think also about specific components – that way you can learn more about your situation.

Because all of the Top Twelve features are in general
linked to happiness or unhappiness (that's why they're in
the list), you'll probably rate them all as important to some
degree. So we need to concentrate on the ones which are
more than "moderately important" to you – those scoring 4,
5 or 6. Those job features, the ones you most value, are the
ones you especially need to get right.

Step 4: Put together your job and your wants

Your answers on the three kinds of questionnaires (your job
happiness, your job features, and your job wants) together
point to two key questions (page 50):

Questionnaire 5: Features in your job

(A printable version of this questionnaire is available at www.psypress.com/joyofwork)

Considering all aspects of your job in the past few weeks, please summarize that by placing a circle around the appropriate number in each case below.

		Very much too low	Much too low	Slightly too low	About right	Slightly too high	Much too high	Very much too high
					The amount of the feature available to me is:			
1	Personal influence (What you can change)	1	2	3	4	5	6	7
2	Using your abilities (Applying your strengths)	1	2	3	4	5	6	7
3	Demands and goals (What you have to do)	1	2	3	4	5	6	7
4	Variety (Different activities)	1	2	3	4	5	6	7
5	Clear requirements and outlook (Not too much uncertainty)	1	2	3	4	5	6	7
6	Social contacts (Enough and good dealings with others)	1	2	3	4	5	6	7

		Very much too low	Much too low	Slightly too low	About right	Quite acceptable	Very acceptable	Extremely acceptable
7	Money (Getting paid)	1	2	3	4	5	6	7
8	Adequate physical setting (Working conditions)	1	2	3	4	5	6	7
9	A valued role (Social consequences and self-worth)	1	2	3	4	5	6	7
10	Supportive supervision (Helpful in getting the job done)	1	2	3	4	5	6	7
11	Good career outlook (Security and prospects)	1	2	3	4	5	6	7
12	Fair treatment (For employees and others)	1	2	3	4	5	6	7

Today's date:

- Are you unhappy enough in your job to want to try to do something about it (Questionnaires 1 and 2)?
- If so, which job aspects are both troublesome (Questionnaires 3 and 5) and very important to you (Questionnaire 4)?

Remember you may also want to ask about particular aspects of some of the features. And it's important to view the situation over a period of weeks; if you're feeling particularly high or particularly low at the moment, you're going to get a distorted snapshot.

Second, look at yourself

The next steps take us in a different direction. We've emphasized that happiness comes from within yourself, as well as from the world outside. You may remember the lines of poetry quoted in Chapter 8:

Happiness depends, as Nature shows,
Less on exterior things than most suppose.

So it's essential to think also about factors beyond the "exterior things" in your job. We'll have a look at those now.

Step 5: Ask about your happiness baseline

One "interior" source of happiness or unhappiness is your own personality. As we said in Chapter 7, people all have characteristic levels of generally positive or negative feelings about things, and their reactions to events are affected by these. An individual's feelings are fairly similar when they switch and change jobs, because that's the way people are. If you're a generally cheerful person, the odds are you'll be cheerful in whatever job you have. And the same principle works for those who are less cheerful.

It follows that job reactions don't depend on job features alone. They also come from the general outlook of the person involved and the fact that across a period of time everyone moves back towards a personal happiness baseline. So you must ask yourself: would I feel happier in a few months time if a certain job feature changed now, or am I instead likely to feel much as I do now?

Writing that question down was a pushover compared to answering it. A crucial factor is the magnitude of change: something that is hugely different from now can have a continuing effect on you, but the benefits from a small or moderate change probably won't last long. It's often helpful to reflect about previous similar changes if you can think of some. How long did the impact last? Was it long enough to be worth the hassle that went into getting it?

This general point may seem a bit negative and pessimistic: surely we should keep striving to make things better for ourselves and our family, even if we'll eventually slip back towards our previous feelings? Well, yes, we certainly should, but the point about Step 5 is to ask you to be realistic. One alternative is to live with something that is OK but less than perfect, recognizing that much of life is like that. You can cause yourself a great deal of difficulty and anxiety trying to alter your job, only to find that a minor change doesn't much alter your happiness in the longer term.

So reflect on your baseline level. For instance, have you been similarly happy or unhappy in other jobs? Are you about as unhappy in your job as you are in your social life? Or is this job different – making you miserable although you're generally quite cheerful? That can be an important sign. You should strive to become happier at work, but do recognize that your feelings are unlikely to shift enormously in the longer term unless changes in your situation have been very great. Aim high, but don't expect a huge transformation.

OK, let's look again at the key question in Step 4:

- Are you unhappy enough in your job to want to try to do something about it?

As a result of Step 5, this now becomes:

- Recognizing that you are likely to return towards your happiness baseline after a while, are you unhappy enough in your job to want to try to do something about it?

You may feel it's best to accept what you've got; every situation has its downside. You may then prefer not to get into the actions suggested later in Step 8. However, another kind of change may instead be possible and helpful – maybe you could alter your typical ways of thinking. Let's look at those next.

Step 6: Ask about your thinking styles

Chapter 8 showed how feelings are in part due to how you interpret and process what happens to you. We looked at mental comparisons with other people, thoughts about what might otherwise have happened, and the importance of your prior expectations. In brief, some people think in ways which make them more unhappy than they would otherwise be.

You'll make yourself feel worse if you regularly think about other people who are in a better position than yourself, if you keep reflecting how much better things could have been, or if you start with unrealistic, inflated expectations. Happy people often do the opposite –notice how others are worse-off and how things could have been less good, and set themselves only modest (but often challenging!) expectations. So two people in the same job situation can feel quite differently about it – they have different thinking styles, interpreting the same world in different ways.

As part of your efforts to increase happiness you clearly need to examine your usual styles of this kind. Do you generally think along lines that will make you feel less happy than you might be? It's sometimes difficult to analyze yourself in these respects, and we have four suggestions.

First, you could reflect on a recent unpleasant event. How did you think about that as you reacted to it? Did you bring to mind the good things you've missed or other people who didn't have your misfortune? Those comparisons (we called them "upward" in Chapter 8) serve to emphasize your own relative lack of success and are likely to depress your mood.

Second, you might ponder the way you approach new activities. Do you often have high expectations that turn out to be unrealistic? We realize it's difficult to decide what is and what is not "unrealistic" and that strong positive expectations are necessary to keep up motivation – sometimes they're essential. But some individuals routinely have hopes for a situation which are so high that they are almost certain to be shattered. No successful actor has *really* expected to get steady work, pleased though they may be when it arrives; if they had expected permanent employment they wouldn't have started, realizing that they were doomed to fail.

Don't forget that expectations include some about yourself. A major source of unhappiness is a habit of expecting yourself to reach targets that are higher than is reasonable or which require unachievably swift progress. For instance, by unrealistically promising "I'll do that by Friday," you could be causing yourself (and your work colleagues) a lot of difficulty later. It's important to include your typical expectancy styles when thinking about the ways in which your happiness is affected by yourself as well as by what happens to you.

Third, pause in the course of some future episodes and reflect about your thought processes. What sort of mental comparisons have you made, against other people and against other situations? How high were your expectations, and how realistic do you now believe them to have been? Would alternative interpretations as suggested above have made a difference to your happiness?

Fourth, it's a good idea sometimes to watch and listen to work colleagues and other people in your life: how do they think and react in situations like your own? Are they making upward or downward comparisons? Do their mental spectacles lead them to think in more positive ways than you do?

Overall then, Step 6 requires you to reflect on the ways in which your typical thinking styles may shape how you feel. This can be interesting even if you're not planning to change things: how do you generally operate in those ways? As part of your self-examination, you might look again at themes in Chapter 8.

Step 7: Identify possible changes to your thinking

Given that both your personal baseline (Step 5) and your thinking styles (Step 6) can affect your happiness or unhappiness, you may need to consider possible ways to change those aspects of you rather than making changes to your job. They aren't easy to shift, but we'll make some suggestions in Step 9. Right now there's an initial question to ask yourself: do you want or need to try?

To answer that, you may need a bit of ruthlessness. Most of us are a bit defensive when we think about our possible limitations. We often maintain self-esteem by not noticing less-than-desirable behaviors or thoughts, or we seek to justify to ourselves what we have done. That's perfectly healthy, but you need to see through mental defenses of that kind if you are to learn about your thinking styles. One approach is to imagine yourself as other people might see you. (Or you could ask someone, as long as you don't mind a less-than-wonderful answer.) From the standpoint of an uninvolved observer, are there aspects of your mental approach which might lead you to become more unhappy than you need to be? Do other people sometimes think you are overly pessimistic or optimistic?

You may have got some ideas from Step 6 activities as you checked your approach to things. Did you spot issues which may need some work? Step 7 asks you to pick out those aspects of your behaviors and thinking styles which you'd like to change.

This issue is sometimes viewed in terms of personal responsibility. Just as you are partly responsible for your physical fitness – there are actions you can take to make yourself fitter – you have some responsibility for your mental well-being. Your well-being belongs to you; as its owner, you should look after it. There's undoubtedly a limit on how far you can actively change your feelings, but you can often make some difference. It's partly up to you.

So it's important to consider how far you see yourself more as the victim of circumstances and how far you view your happiness as a personal responsibility. You'll realize by now that we like to emphasize the second of those, but for you the decision is of course your own. If you take on board the idea of some personal responsibility, it's essential to look hard at possible changes to your thinking. Some suggestions are in the next chapter.

10

Worth a try?

Right. It's time for the nitty gritty of actions and practical steps. The last chapter focused on the features of your job that most affect your happiness and summarized your feelings about those, including the degree you value each one in an ideal job (Steps 1 to 4). And Steps 5 to 7 aimed to help you understand your thinking habits and why they make you feel the way you do. The chapter may also have led you to some possible targets for action in respect of both your job (Step 4) and your ways of thinking (Step 7).

Third, consider what might be done

So let's move on to the third set of issues. We'll first look at possible actions in your job (Step 8) – aiming to increase happiness by changing job conditions. Then we'll suggest some ways to modify your mental approach – aiming to increase happiness by changing you rather than your job (Step 9).

Step 8: Ask about ways to improve your job

Can you yourself improve what happens at work so you feel better about it? That's going to depend on a lot of things. Some readers have enough discretion to make alterations they want, but for others that can be impossible: "you versus the world" (for instance, in the face of an international economic recession) or "you versus autocratic management" (when dictatorial bosses stifle any sort of attempt).

But don't write off your own autonomy just yet. It's worth spending some time thinking about what you would like to happen, and then exploring some possible routes in that direction.

Steps 1 to 4 should have helped you understand the kind of job in which you have a good chance of happiness. You would especially enjoy work which has medium-to-high levels of those features of the Top Twelve and their components which you rated in Questionnaire 4 as particularly valued.

In many cases, several of your job features will be OK, and the problem is restricted to only a few aspects. For dealing with those you can of course either remain where you are or you could move to a different job. Moving will be more difficult or more simple depending on whether you're reading this book in the middle of a recession or after a recovery. For our purposes we'll assume that moving is at least a possibility. Let's look separately at activities for those staying or going.

STAYING WHERE YOU ARE

A job develops gradually over the years as activities are put together and modified to fit better with other jobs and with changes in the environment. For example, someone in marketing ten years ago would have had a reasonably traditional job; nowadays in many sectors they'd be involved with social media such as Facebook, Twitter and others. And think how other jobs have altered in recent decades to keep up with advancing information technology.

Part of the change comes from individuals themselves, as they shift job activities slightly to suit their preferences. Sometimes it's because people in a group allocate tasks between themselves to suit their different strengths. For whatever reason, jobs rarely stand still so that after a period of time two people's jobs with the same title are unlikely to have exactly the same content.

That content comes from three sources – your managers, yourself, your colleagues. If it's to be changed, the ideal outcome is one of win–win–win for those three contributors. In addition to the middle one (yourself), we need also to think about bosses and colleagues; will they also "win" if you succeed in changing things in your favor?

First, consider what might be possible by yourself. An obvious place to start has been described in Chapter 5 as "job crafting" – informal changes to job activities so they better suit your strengths and needs. A shop-floor worker might decide to train the newcomers, or a marketing employee might take on event-planning tasks. Look again at the features that you don't enjoy. For instance, if your level of variety (feature 4) is too low, can you gradually find ways to break up repetition? Perhaps you can do things in different sequences on different days, intersperse some boring tasks with other activities, or replace some mundane approaches with others you find more stimulating.

In some cases, maybe you could arrange a specific short-term assignment to other activities, both to use your own expertise and to enhance your happiness features overall. If possible, seek out activities and projects of the kind you're good at. Finding extra ways to use and build on your personal strengths will make you feel better – and probably increase your job effectiveness. That's a powerful message when you're arguing a position to managers.

For inadequate social contacts (6), perhaps you can make special efforts. You might devote extra time to helping others or set up some informal activities (a departmental football team? something less energetic?). The people at Innocent Drinks, which previously employed our interviewee Bronte Blomhoj (see Chapter 4), set up a drum club among other things. No matter how wild your idea might seem at first, it might just work.

Whatever you do, don't trust too much in a "big bang" approach; you may have to improve things gradually by trial and error over quite a time. Even if it's your own company, how often have you seen a "new broom" approach fail or watched other companies flailing around as people tire of the latest in a long series of so-called innovations? And, as well as trying to adjust some aspects that are negative, also focus on your job's plus-points. How might some of those be made even better for you?

Job-crafting activities can sometimes be thought of in terms of what Harvard University psychologist Tal Ben-Shahar has described as the "MPS process" – concerned with "meaning," "pleasure" and "strengths" (as introduced in Chapter 3). He suggests you ask three questions: "What gives me meaning in my job? In other words, what provides me with a sense of purpose?", "What gives me pleasure? In other words, what do I enjoy doing?", and "What are my strengths? In other words, what am I good at?"[1]

For happiness in a job and elsewhere, he urges us to look beyond merely the "pleasure" aspects (the ones you enjoy) and try to maximize all three of those. Can you identify areas where you could build on your job's potential for "meaning" and where you can better exploit your strengths?

The latter have been brought together by University of Pennsylvania Professor Martin Seligman into 24 "signature strengths" – the ones that are particularly yours. Illustrations are: love of learning, originality, social and emotional intelligence, persistence, and leadership. See, for example, the web-site www.authentichappiness.org. Given that activities based on signature strengths are good for us, it's worth aiming for informal changes in your job to find a way to use some of yours more than before.

Whether you focus on "pleasure" alone or also cover "meaning" and "strengths," it's worth trying out some of these job-crafting ideas. You may have more informal influence than you realize, adjusting what you do quietly without making a fuss about it. However, altering your job is like dieting – it takes time. Don't rush; it's often best to move by small steps rather than trying a big jump. Your employer may welcome minor innovations that don't seem risky or troublesome but which could eventually add up to something special.

Personal modifications of these kinds are probably more common among managers and professional workers, for whom flexibility is generally expected. Some of those may also have received personalized treatment in the contracts negotiated on joining the organization – specifying for them alone some preferred activities, time allocations, work locations, and so on. Those sort of personalized deals are clearly great if you can get them, but they can cause problems of comparability with colleagues who are treated differently.

Professor Denise Rousseau of Carnegie Mellon University in Pittsburgh, USA, has made a special study of what she calls "idiosyncratic deals" or "i-deals" for short.[2] We don't suggest that many workers can negotiate an explicit agreement just for themselves, but we do believe that most have some potential to shape what they do more than they may realize.

Professor Rousseau points out that it is important to lay the groundwork by checking out possibilities, look around your own and other organizations (perhaps "benchmarking" is too strong a description, but it gives the idea), and try to build support from your colleagues. That last suggestion applies generally: in many of the activities in this chapter remember that you are not alone – check out other people's views and preferences.

Also as part of your attempts to modify your job activities, it's worth looking at "self-help" procedures available in books and on the internet. Prominent are ways to improve your management of time, so you more effectively achieve your targets as well as reducing your feelings of overload tension. Some of those procedures might help you, for example in creating task lists, identifying clearer priorities, and better prioritizing and scheduling your activities. Improvements in those directions can be helpful not only in reducing job hassles and strain but also in providing satisfaction from the smooth achievement of job goals. Other self-help ideas concern ways to manage your feelings, without altering the job. We'll look at those when we get to Step 9.

So far we've dealt with possible "wins" for you. Second in the win–win–win framework described earlier, what about a potential "win" for the organization that may come from adjusting tasks to suit you better? Let's be clear: we're not advocating private routes to cheating, slacking, rule-breaking or other anti-employer activities. But research studies have shown that improvements to job content can

lead to workers' greater engagement with their organization, yielding potential "wins" for both. So some informal
job crafting can help a company's effectiveness and profitability as well as staff's well-being.

Watch out, though – you don't want your idea to end up
yielding a win–win–lose pattern – for your organization,
yourself and your colleagues respectively. It can be the case
that what is good for you is bad for some colleagues. So you
often need to develop a joint approach. Can you and your
colleagues come to an arrangement that helps all of you?
Take your time over that, or your proposed change to your
tasks might seem to be suggesting that the others aren't
really up to the job. But do think about it.

Here's a start for you. Concentrating on the Top Twelve
issues that are in the danger zones of Questionnaire 5 for
you (pages 148–149), what do your workmates think of
those? Is there some way you can do some job crafting
between yourselves? For instance, informal job rotation
might be possible, with colleagues swapping between
activities to introduce variety through different kinds of
work from time to time. Or maybe you can exchange some
tasks between colleagues to better suit their individual
preferences and skills.

We realize that for some readers this will seem
impossible, since their job appears to offer no opportunities
of that kind or their colleagues don't want to know. Nevertheless, please stand back and think as widely as you can.
Work through the Top Twelve and their components and
spend time on each one: what win–win–win changes might
be possible in principle?

Inevitably many valuable job modifications depend on
the involvement of managers. They have power to make
things happen and they also have a broader view of implications in combination with other jobs. Managers' perspectives necessarily include concerns about expenditure and
potential negative impacts elsewhere in the organization.
For example, one problem that can arise from giving
more personal influence (feature 1) to some workers is that
it sometimes has to be taken away from someone else.
The losers (supervisors, for instance) may not only be

dissatisfied but also reckon they are now less effective, perhaps being undermined in their activities. (In some cases, they could instead be given additional new responsibilities. Think about that possibility.)

Although some job-crafting changes can be achieved by individual workers alone, larger modifications usually require a joint approach coordinated through management. For example, working practices might be changed across an entire section, and organizational support for new learning and skill development is often needed to provide additional expertise. At the very least, you could do with some discussion between you and your manager about the content of your job and how it might be improved. It's extremely sad and usually counterproductive that some managers never ask their staff about possible changes which could help the company. Can you find a way to arrange such a discussion?

Many managers are so busy that they don't stop to think about the well-being consequences of their decisions. Others have considered some issues in this book but don't see the point of looking for job changes to increase worker happiness, especially in difficult times when other practical issues are more pressing. We recognize that, if short-term company survival is at risk, then that needs to be the top priority. However, it's also essential to take a longer-term view, and then the well-being of staff is of the greatest importance.

This is especially obvious if changes can lead not only to increased happiness but also to improvements in effectiveness and profitability – and they can do that. As we discussed in Chapter 3, a good approach is sometimes to talk in terms of "morale" rather than "happiness." Good morale is a form of happiness that is linked to effective work.

However, even in straightforward economic conditions, a general worry stops many managers in their tracks: if workers' problems are openly discussed, management will be expected to do something about them, and that's going to lead to upheaval and difficulty – a Pandora's Box effect. That's an understandable concern, and a possible response has been implied at the end of the previous paragraph – view the issue in terms of morale and its improvement.

It's best to start happiness/morale discussions firmly on the basis that financial restrictions are tight so that there has to be a guarantee of at least present levels of productivity and preferably a good chance of increasing those. Mind you, we've shown that worker well-being and performance can go together, so we'd hope for productivity improvements rather than merely no-change from these discussions. (Don't forget that attracting and retaining staff come in here; research shows that low well-being increases staff turnover with its considerable hassle, inefficiency and expense. And it's linked to absenteeism.) If you are a manager, please consider giving this morale-and-productivity approach a try, perhaps first in a small way with one group of staff.

As well as initiating discussions of that kind, managers can help employees' well-being by considering happiness as a factor in their strategic and tactical decision-making. We hope that some readers in positions of influence will review the Top Twelve features in their organization (or their bit of it) and look for possible improvements in general terms as well as in particular cases. How does morale look in the company (or section etc.) as a whole, how much attention is paid generally to the themes of Chapters 5 and 6, and should some policies be changed to focus more on morale and its causes? As we've emphasized, greater employee well-being can be good for the financial bottom-line as well as being a worthwhile target in its own right.

It's also important to reflect on the well-being implications of your organization's planning process in respect of equipment and procedures. Analyses of system options in terms of costs and benefits are traditionally restricted to financial considerations. That's clearly a primary concern, but it's necessary also to examine options' likely impact on the way people will have to work. Activities entailed by a design decision can have unintended consequences for low or high productivity and associated staff happiness/morale. So decisions' follow-on implications for job content need to be included when you're planning equipment and systems, as well as issues of a financial kind. Perhaps you could try out this broader planning perspective, again perhaps initially in a small way?

The widespread application of information-technology and computer-based communication systems has encouraged many managers to reduce their concern for staff welfare in those domains. It is easy to be blinded by technical expertise, fantastic equipment and apparently limitless system possibilities, so that the humble user gets left out of new designs and processes of installation. Users' opinions are rarely sought, despite the fact that they are the ones who know about a system in reality rather than in theory. One very important way for managers to improve many workers' happiness as well as overall efficiency is to insist on system designs that are human-centered as well as focused on the technology. Quite often that will make it clear that bigger systems are not always the better.

Ask yourself how many times you've heard employees in organizations where you're a customer complaining about their new computer system, or performing poorly because they haven't been adequately trained to use such a system. They're no happier than you are that they're unable to get their job right. In designing new information systems and job content the opinions and needs of users should always be considered.

Junior and middle managers often feel hemmed in by company procedures and expectations, so the trail again often leads to the top. Initiatives by senior managers are vital, both in terms of setting a personal example and launching programs of change linked to the framework presented here.

One restricted focus for possible managerial action is of course on job feature 10: supportive supervision. Let's stress again that this is formulated here to include effectiveness as well as happiness. What can your organization do to improve this feature? First, do you know about the likely well-being impact of local managers' styles of interaction with subordinates? Are individuals fair and considerate as well as firm, hard-working and focused on effectiveness? Are there signs that some may slip into bullying from time to time? What can you do in problem cases? Where in the organization do you see "best practice" in supportive supervision and how can you build on that? As with other features, there are often no easy answers, but if you believe as we do that staff happiness ("morale" if you prefer) is crucial then these issues must be shifted up the agenda.

TIME FOR A MOVE?

In the last few pages we've considered possible ways to make changes to the job you are in at the moment. In those cases, the assumption is that you'll be staying there. However, sometimes the gap between what you want and what you have is so great and so unlikely to be reduced that it's a good idea to look elsewhere. Let's review that option, recognizing that the state of the labor market can make a big difference. If times are very hard, your possibilities are obviously limited. (But you can plan in advance for when an upturn comes.)

Many books and web-sites present detailed suggestions on how to choose a job and manage your career. Take a look at some of those if you might feel better somewhere else. But watch out. Plenty of web-sites out there are recruitment sites which get paid when they get you a new job. That's OK if you're sure about your direction, but if you're looking for career guidance try to stick to sites that have no vested interest, at least at first. After that, by all means let the recruiters make their money if that helps you as well.

However, within the framework of a book focusing on the factors which matter to you, here are some points about moving from one job to another. First, it is entirely sensible to want to do that sometimes; both you and your job can shift over time. Second, however, it's clearly essential to be realistic: often there is no immediate alternative, particularly when the economy starts to tighten up. You may have literally to "make the best of a bad job," trying to build in some changes to your present role as described earlier in the chapter. Third, your prospects of a good job change are greater if you prepare yourself.

It's often essential to avoid a short-term view, instead looking at possible development opportunities and maybe obtaining additional qualifications which will be helpful in the future. This means researching different job areas, checking what experience and skills you need, talking with people already working in those fields, looking into local and remote learning courses available, and maybe talking to your employers about what might be done. Researching for the book *Britain's top employers*, coauthor Guy Clapperton learned of a Pret A Manger employee who had been funded by the company to attend teacher training college. She left her job after the course, but was more motivated while she was there – and of course recommends the company to everyone who wants to work in retail.

Procedures in the last chapter may help you to better define what you should aim for. In that respect you particularly need to be clear about your work values – the personal importance to you of particular aspects of a job (see Questionnaire 4, pages 138–139). And also think about the "MPS process" described earlier in this chapter – reviewing alternative jobs for their potential "meaning" as well as "pleasure" to you and how far they permit use of your "strengths." Try to define the kind of job that would make you happy in those terms. And do think widely; that better job could be very different from your present one.

That point is emphasized in Richard Bolles's long-established *What color is your parachute?*,[3] first appearing in 1970 and regularly updated since then. (The 2009 edition is subtitled "Job-hunting in hard times.") Overlap with the present framework is through Richard Bolles's emphasis on people's favorite transferable skills – "the basic building blocks of your work" (page 210).

He presents psychologist Sidney Fine's account of skills when working with "data" or "people" or "things," and provides a 100-item questionnaire about different skills which may be linked to different jobs. As we have emphasized, it's important to know yourself in the areas of this book – your work values, sources of personal meaning, and strengths – as well as in your more obvious needs about a job's geographical area, wage rate, required hours and so on.

Finally in this section we mustn't forget your nonjob activities. What you do outside work is obviously crucial to your global happiness and unhappiness. If you are stuck in a rotten job which seems difficult to change, or even if your work has attractive as well as negative features, perhaps you can boost your overall well-being by adjusting some nonjob aspects of life.

In part this could involve a change of relative emphasis: downgrade the personal significance of your work (don't immerse yourself so much, lower your sights, strive less) and instead pay greater attention to family and leisure activities. Another way of saying this is to talk about "work–life balance"; sometimes the only way to improve that is by cutting back on one of the two roles – you can't do everything. (Yes, we agree that cutting back on a job may be a pushover in theory but not easy when there are mouths to feed.)

Some people tolerate a disliked job simply as a necessary nuisance, while throwing themselves enthusiastically into other kinds of activity. Other people take one element of a job as compensation for the grind – think of actors who do commercials (or trashy films if they're a bit higher in the pecking order), in order to be able to afford the low-paid theater work and independent movies they really relish. Would some sort of compromise like that be appropriate for you?

You can think about possible nonwork activities in terms of the framework of this book, identifying gaps and possible targets. Most of the Top Twelve job features are also important in life as a whole. We identified those in Chapter 4 as the "Needed Nine," and they are the bases of global happiness as well as happiness in jobs. It may be useful to apply Steps 2 and 3 (in Chapter 9) to your life as a whole – profiling your overall situation in respect of features 1 to 9 (Step 2) and summarizing the importance to you of particular features from that set (Step 3). You could then aim to improve your nonjob happiness by targeting those aspects of life you specially value but are currently lacking. By simultaneously reducing the importance you attach to your job, your overall happiness has a good chance of being improved.

Step 9: Ask about ways to change your outlook

We've emphasized that happiness and unhappiness come from within you as well as from your environment. So it's also essential to check your outlook and typical styles of thinking, summarized in the last chapter as Steps 5 and 6. Can you do anything to alter the way you view the world, even if you can't change the world itself?

The personality factors shown in Chapter 7 to most affect happiness were Emotional Stability (otherwise described as low Neuroticism), Extraversion and Conscientiousness. It's not easy to change long-term personality dispositions, but you might be able to look at and alter some of the behaviors and thoughts which underlie them. All personality traits involve linked habitual activities. For instance, people with high scores on Neuroticism scales are likely to repeatedly spend time looking for problems and reflecting on possible reasons and solutions. They may also inappropriately blame themselves when things go wrong.

We know it's difficult, but if you're that sort of a person try stopping negative thoughts as soon as they start. Even better, aim to replace them with ideas that are positive. Maybe that project did go wrong, but previous failures have been followed by some positive outcomes, and anyway you're as good as the other people! Generally, try to shift negative mental activities into other channels, for instance more readily accepting things without thinking too much about them. Can you identify a few kinds of your harmful thoughts which could be shifted just a little? And find some more optimistic ideas which are personally meaningful for you.

So a more Neurotic personality (defined earlier) may be difficult to change overall, but people with that personality can modify particular behaviors and thoughts. That's also the case for the personality factors of Conscientiousness and Extraversion. Setting yourself new goals (an instance of behavior by a Conscientious personality) not only takes your mind off negative thoughts (because you're busy getting on with things) but may also lead to enjoyable outcomes. Similarly, increasing some activities with other people (one part of being Extraverted) has been shown to reduce unhappiness. (It's often difficult to get started in that respect, but research makes it clear that the effort is worthwhile.) The general point is that, if your unhappiness is partly a reflection of your personality traits, why not look for particular trait-related behaviors or thoughts which you can change or initiate more easily? You may feel anxious at first in the new situations, but there's a good chance that persistence will yield rewards.

Personality traits also have a general impact on happiness in terms of your "fit" with your job. For example, if you are strongly extraverted you will be unhappy in solitary work roles that prevent interaction with other people. Here's a retail shop assistant who has decided to move into a graphic design job. "My talent lies in the creative side of the brain. I'm basically an introspective person. Which is good for problem-solving . . . but not the best for dealing with bitchy customers. Customer 'relations' doesn't come naturally to me."[4]

Turning to particular thoughts that promote unhappiness or happiness, Chapter 8 identified "upward" mental comparisons (with people or alternative situations that are better than yours) as a regular source of problems. Some people are a bit hooked on that kind of thinking. Yet we know from research studies that people who repeatedly compare their situation against more desirable ones are unhappier than others. They are often struggling to "keep up with the Joneses" or to reach that "grass which is greener on the other side" (it rarely is). Try persuading yourself instead to view aspects of your situation in other comparative ways: which of your job features are better than some other people's, better than they used to be, better than you expected, better than they could have been, or how are the bad features balanced by good ones?

It's worth practicing downward comparisons when something negative happens. You get made redundant – but some people lose their jobs without a redundancy payoff. Maybe your child misbehaves – but don't forget that some people are unable to have children. Of course, you can push these ideas too far, into the absurd (you've just hit your thumb with a hammer but it's OK because there's a bloke in Africa who's just been mauled by a lion), but as long as the possibilities are close to home and realistic they may help you. The self-help books often describe that in terms of appreciating how lucky you are. Try describing and emphasizing the features in your job which you're lucky to have in comparison with other people.

We've also looked at problems caused by inflated expectations. People who anticipate really great success are more likely to be disappointed by failure than those who anticipate a bit less. This is a question of two kinds of expectation: about events that occur largely beyond our control (those are going to happen whatever you do), and about the personal targets we have set for ourselves. Thinking about what goes on in your job, could it be helpful to lower your personal expectations of those kinds, at least in some areas? All the evidence says it would help.

In general, then, you may be able to increase your happiness at work by adjusting some personality-linked behaviors and by modifying some thinking styles. Perhaps you could look again at Chapters 7 and 8 to find some personal action points?

Several of the themes in those chapters also occur in self-help books and presentations that make no mention of jobs. Those books can contain a lot of useful ideas that deserve attention in work settings. Many of their suggestions boil down to a general recommendation to emphasize the positive (or how lucky you are – see above). And it's clear that happier people have a more optimistic view of the world, both seeing things as more pleasant when they occur and also more expecting that future developments will also be good. Is it possible for unhappy people (including unhappy workers) to change the way they look at the world in those respects?

American popular culture has long urged that optimistic shift. Jerome Kern's 1920 song has suggested to millions of people over nearly a century that:

A heart full of joy and gladness
Will always banish sadness and strife.

So always look for the silver lining,
And try to find the sunny side of life.

In 1950s America, Norman Vincent Peale made a huge impact through his ideas about "the power of positive thinking." Pieces of advice included "believe in yourself," "break the worry habit," "stop fuming and fretting," and "don't believe in the prospect of defeat." He also stressed the value of prayer, and it's worth mentioning that people with religious affiliations do tend on average to be more happy than others. (In part this difference can be based on different beliefs and thoughts. However, note that membership of a church also often leads to personal and social activities which increase some of life's Needed Nine features.)

More recent self-help guides add details to some of Peale's ideas, nowadays often taking the line that it's necessary to "challenge unhelpful thoughts." They increasingly base suggestions on procedures of that kind drawn from short-term cognitive behavior therapy (CBT) as used with patients with anxiety, depression, and other mental illnesses. This is a brief "talking" treatment, with a focus on how someone thinks about what happens to him or her and ways in which harmful thoughts may be changed.

Research has shown that tackling unhelpful thoughts can be very effective in the clinic, and similar thought-adjusting procedures can also be useful for nonmedical problems at work and elsewhere. A general theme is that we go through life partly on auto-pilot, reacting to situations through our own habitual routines. Some of those routines are bad for well-being. So let's try to cancel out automatic routines which are negative and replace them with positive thoughts and behaviors that can help us to be more happy.

What are the negative thoughts which are targeted in cognitive behavior therapy and related approaches? Typical sources of difficulty include:

- overgeneralization: coming to a general conclusion – usually a negative one – from a single piece of evidence (e.g. "I made a mess of that job. I never do things properly")

- concentrating on the negative: ignoring or down-grading positive aspects of a situation (e.g. "my annual appraisal told me I can't get along with colleagues," when it merely made specific improvement suggestions within an overall positive appraisal)
- believing you are at fault: taking responsibility for something negative that you haven't caused (e.g. "my boss is really irritable today. I must have done something wrong" or "I lost my job because I'm no good," when bad financial conditions caused widespread redundancies).

Of course, we all veer in a negative direction from time to time, but it's hard to disagree with the suggestion that less negative thinking would mean more happiness. Focusing on your job, try mentally challenging some of your own negative thoughts of the kinds illustrated here. Generally, aim to work on the basis that "this problem isn't because of me."

The great majority of do-it-yourself books are based on authors' experiences and beliefs rather than systematic evidence. However, in the last two decades psychologists have carried out experiments to learn about the different things people do to cheer themselves up when they're unhappy. You "do" things both by your actions and also by your thoughts, so we're interested in both of those. Actions may be aimed directly at what you see as the problem (for instance, trying to change something that's troubling you) or they can instead provide diversions or distractions (take a break, do some cooking, go to the pub, or whatever). Similarly, mental activities can be of those two kinds – either more directed at the cause of your unhappiness (for instance, thinking about how a problem might be solved or how to look at things in a different way) or more diversionary (recalling happier times or thinking about another topic).

In practice, these general coping strategies get mixed up with each other, as you do and think a lot of things. So it's not surprising that research hasn't pointed to a single "best" approach. There is evidence that women more often talk to other people when they need cheering up and that men see more value in being active (for instance, in hobbies, sports and so on); also that most people find that chatting with friendly colleagues can make a difference (back to "social support" again). However, situations and problems differ widely (perhaps you haven't got any "friendly colleagues" to chat with), so it's not sensible to look for overall solutions.

Instead, some researchers have set out to evaluate more specific self-help procedures and to maximize their particular effectiveness. We've mentioned themes of cognitive behavior therapy and signature strengths, both extensively researched, and now turn to a series of experiments on self-help "interventions" which might enhance well-being. These usually compare groups of people who have been asked to try out different activities and thoughts and for whom happiness levels are measured before and after the experiment: do the people adopting one approach end up happier than the ones doing something different?

Several key questions still have to be answered. For instance, if a self-help activity is found to be effective, how long do its happiness benefits last? How often should someone apply it (repeating the same effortful activity soon gets tedious)? How willing are people to stick with it? Recognizing that more answers are needed, Professor Sonja Lyubomirsky of the University of California has brought together current knowledge into 12 key "happiness activities." These have rarely been applied in job situations, but their effectiveness in general suggests that unhappy workers should give them a try.[5]

Some of the activities probably won't appeal to you, and you can leave those on one side. The idea is that people should select only the ones they like. Illustrations are:

- Expressing gratitude and "counting your blessings." You can sometimes feel better by simply writing down some aspects of your life (or your job, in our case) for which you are grateful. Other happiness-increasing activities include telling people (either in a face-to-face chat or in a letter) that you are grateful for something they have done. Have any colleagues or family members helped you in your work-life recently? We often feel uncomfortable about making public our grateful feelings, but doing so can yield several personal benefits – emphasizing positive aspects of your life, bolstering self-esteem, and strengthening social relationships.

- Avoiding "overthinking." That term is often used to describe excessive rumination about yourself and your situation. When you feel down-hearted, it is certainly sensible to focus on possible reasons and solutions, but those thoughts can go too far. Research as well as common sense has shown how continued self-rumination can make things worse, digging for yourself an even deeper hole of depression and producing a distorted, pessimistic picture of reality.[6]

Although job activities (like those in life more generally) can sometimes be upsetting, it's essential to stop dwelling on them and their possible causes. Along the lines of cognitive behavior therapy (above), negative thoughts need to be redirected into neutral or positive themes. For some people that is extremely difficult, and none of us finds it easy. One approach is to focus on particular kinds of negative idea and shift your attention along the lines suggested in Chapter 8. For instance, if your self-reflections include a lot of "upward" comparisons ("things could be so much better"), look for ways in which "things could be a lot worse."

- Investing in social connections. People who increase their friendly social contacts are known to become happier. There are several reasons for that. Social contact itself is needed to reduce feelings of loneliness, but in addition other people provide useful ideas and information as well as making comforting suggestions when you have problems. One valuable social activity is being kind to people. We don't want to sound preachy, but showing compassion and contributing to others can benefit the doer as well as the recipient, increasing feelings of self-worth, leading to more positive views of people, and creating pleasant relationships as others respond in a positive way. "Do unto others as . . ." and other such phrases!

More generally, although it's tempting to keep a low profile when you're feeling down, nurturing social relationships is known to enhance feelings of well-being.

That requires both time and motivation, so you might have to think how those can be increased. Can your job activities be adjusted in some ways to build in time to show interest in your colleagues and discuss with them events of the day and currently troublesome issues?

Social support can contribute directly to your handling of negative job features. For example, if you have a bullying boss or are concerned about an excessive workload, it can help you to discuss those with colleagues; sometimes it is indeed the case that "a problem shared is a problem halved." We emphasized that in Chapter 3's section "You are not alone" (page 33). Spouses, partners, friends and others outside your workplace can be crucial in your mental balance – they're important to you even when you don't realize that. You may fail to change a situation, but you can feel better about it in the light of comfort and encouragement from others, both learning from them how to view things differently and also valuing their sympathy. Or you might find the event put into a new perspective which makes it seem less awful than it did earlier.

Other self-initiated happiness activities described in the book cited in Note 5 at the end of the chapter include committing yourself to goals, learning to forgive, cultivating optimism, and taking care of your body. The last of these is of particular importance, because being worse physically goes along with feeling bad about your situation and a lack of energy to solve your problems. Research studies comparing groups of people following different exercise regimes show clearly the feel-good benefits of aerobic activities as well as their benefits of a physical kind. And we all know how lack of sleep blunts our thinking and feeling. Feeling good physically really does help you to feel better mentally.

Steps 8 and 9 (changing job features and changing yourself) come together in our final suggestion. You can sometimes alter the way you think about key job characteristics. There is often scope for differences of opinion about the facts of a situation or how that should be evaluated. Those differences arise not only from people's own perspectives (as we've been discussing); they also come because we often rely on what other people say about a situation. Your happiness or unhappiness can come from others' opinions of what is the "right" thing to feel.

Professor Ricky Griffin at the University of Missouri, USA, carried out an experiment to look at how supervisors could influence workers' judgment processes and their accompanying job happiness.[7] For one group of workers, supervisors regularly emphasized in discussions how varied and complicated was their job, but for the other group no such comments were made. Sure enough, although no changes were made to the situation, the first group of workers came to see their jobs as more complex and involving and had a significantly higher level of job satisfaction than the other group. The difference in job well-being came from the viewpoints expressed by supervisors, not from the job itself – that stayed the same. Social influences can be very powerful, and it's essential that you look out for those. Are other people influencing the way you think about your job?

The general point is that thoughts about a job are certainly based on its content, but perceptions are not completely fixed. Two workers might be troubled by bullying and harassment from a colleague ("vitamin" 6b), but one may view the abuser as a pathetic individual whose comments deserve no attention, whereas the other may find it difficult to put that person out of mind. Another example concerns a job's perceived social value (feature 9). Perhaps some tasks that are ordinary or unpleasant can be interpreted in terms of the ways they enrich others' lives. Or working conditions and other key features might be viewed differently through alternative kinds of comparisons as described in Chapter 8, for instance more "downward" comparisons and fewer that are "upward."

That brings us back, one more time, to our overall message. Unhappiness at work derives largely from the Top Twelve features, but it also comes from within yourself. Possible improvements must be sought from both directions. Good luck in your search!

Notes

1 See page 109 of *Happier* (New York: McGraw-Hill, 2007). Themes of this kind linked to "positive psychology" were introduced in Chapter 3 and are expanded later in the present chapter.

2 See Denise M. Rousseau, *I-deals: Idiosyncratic deals employees bargain for themselves*. Armonk, NY: M. E. Sharpe, 2005.

3 Richard N. Bolles, *What color is your parachute?* Berkeley, CA: Ten Speed Press, 2009. An associated web-site offers advice and many internet links, but we would warn against its section on personality testing, which includes many scientifically unacceptable measures: www.jobhuntersbible.com.

4 See page 127 of J. Bowe, M. Bowe, and S. Streeter, *Gig: Americans talk about their jobs* (New York: Three Rivers Press, 2000).

5 Details are set out in Sonja Lyubomirsky's *The how of happiness* (London: Sphere, 2007).

6 Women have been shown to be more liable to self-rumination than men, which may be partly responsible for the higher level of depressed feelings that they report.

7 As in all the previous pages, the book's research content is fully referenced in Peter Warr's academic volume *Work, happiness, and unhappiness* (New York: Routledge, 2007).

Appendix: Some further reading

As described in Chapter 1, academic research underlying this book has been examined in detail in Peter Warr's *Work, happiness, and unhappiness* (New York: Routledge, 2007). That book contains more than a thousand research references, and such detail is inappropriate in the present volume.

Instead, Notes at the end of each chapter have indicated a small number of published sources, and we have selected a few particularly relevant publications for this Appendix. The list below covers a small proportion of the material cited in the 2007 volume and the Notes in this one, and also illustrates some later research studies on which we have drawn.

Chapter 1: Work and happiness: An unlikely mix?

Fredrickson, B. L. (2003). The value of positive emotions. *American Scientist*, *91*, 330–335.

Hardy, G. E., Woods, D., & Wall, T. D. (2003). The impact of psychological distress on absence from work. *Journal of Applied Psychology*, *88*, 306–314.

Judge, T. A., Thoresen, C. J., Bono, J. E., & Patton, G. K. (2001). The job satisfaction-job performance relationship: A qualitative and quantitative review. *Psychological Bulletin*, *127*, 376–407.

Lyubomirsky, S., King, L., & Diener, E. (2005). The benefits of frequent positive affect: Does happiness lead to success? *Psychological Bulletin*, *131*, 803–855.

Patterson, M. J., Warr, P. B., & West, M. A. (2004). Organizational climate and company productivity: The role of employee affect and employee level. *Journal of Occupational and Organizational Psychology, 77*, 193–216.

Thomas, K. (ed.) (1999). *The Oxford book of work.* Oxford, UK: Oxford University Press.

Tsai, W-C., Chen, C-C., & Liu, H-L. (2007). Test of a model linking employee positive moods and task performance. *Journal of Applied Psychology, 92*, 1570–1593.

Chapter 2: Why work?

Jahoda, M. (1982). *Employment and unemployment: A social-psychological analysis.* Cambridge, UK: Cambridge University Press.

McKee-Ryan, F. M., Song, Z., Wanberg, C. R., & Kinicki, A. J. (2005). Psychological and physical well-being during unemployment: A meta-analytic study. *Journal of Applied Psychology, 90*, 53–76.

Paul, K. I., & Moser, K. (2006). Incongruence as an explanation for the negative mental health effects of unemployment: Meta-analytic evidence. *Journal of Occupational and Organizational Psychology, 79*, 595–621.

Warr, P. B. (1987). *Work, unemployment, and mental health.* Oxford, UK: Oxford University Press.

Chapter 3: Feeling good and feeling bad

Carver, C. S. (2001). Affect and the functional bases of behavior: On the dimensional structure of affective experience. *Personality and Social Psychology Review, 5*, 345–356.

Csikszentmihalyi, M. (1997). *Finding flow.* New York: Basic Books.

Isen, A. M. (1999). Positive affect. In T. Dagleish and M. Power (eds.), *Handbook of cognition and emotion* (pp. 521–539). New York: Wiley.

Keyes, C. L. M. (2002). The mental health continuum: From languishing to flourishing in life. *Journal of Health and Social Behavior, 43*, 207–222.

Macey, W. H., & Schneider, B. (2008). The meaning of employee engagement. *Industrial and Organizational Psychology, 1*, 3–30.

Petersen, C., Park, N., & Sweeney, P. J. (2008). Group well-being: Morale from a positive psychology perspective. *Applied Psychology: An International Review, 57*, 19–36.

Russell, J. A. (2003). Core affect and the psychological construction of emotion. *Psychological Review*, *110*, 145–172.

Seligman, M. E. P. (2002). *Authentic happiness*. New York: Free Press.

Tellegen, A., Watson, D., & Clark, L. A. (1999). On the dimensional and hierarchical structure of affect. *Psychological Science*, *10*, 297–303.

Chapter 4: The Needed Nine features

Cummins, R. A. (2000). Personal income and subjective well-being: A review. *Journal of Happiness Studies*, *1*, 133–158.

Iyengar, S. S., & Lepper, M. R. (2000). When choice is demotivating: Can one desire too much of a good thing? *Journal of Personality and Social Psychology*, *79*, 995–1006.

Klumb, P. L., & Lampert, T. (2004). Women, work, and well-being 1950–2000: A review and methodological critique. *Social Science and Medicine*, *58*, 1007–1024.

Warr, P. B., Butcher, V., Robertson, I. T., & Callinan, M. (2004). Older people's well-being as a function of employment, retirement, environmental characteristics and role preference. *British Journal of Psychology*, *95*, 297–324.

Chapter 5: What's in a job? 1. Seeking a happy medium

Baltes, B. B., Bauer, C. C., Bajdo, L. M., & Parker, C. P. (2002). The use of multi-trait-multimethod data for detecting non-linear relationships: The case of psychological climate and job satisfaction. *Journal of Business and Psychology*, *17*, 3–17.

Einarsen, S., Hoel, H., Zapf, D., & Cooper, C. L. (eds.) (2003). *Bullying and emotional abuse in the workplace*. London: Taylor and Francis.

Loher, B. T., Noe, R. A., Moeller, N. L., & Fitzgerald, M. P. (1985). A meta-analysis of the relation of job characteristics to job satisfaction. *Journal of Applied Psychology*, *70*, 280–289.

O'Brien, G. E. (1983). Skill utilization, skill variety and the job characteristics model. *Australian Journal of Psychology*, *35*, 461–468.

Oldham, G. R., & Rotchford, N. L. (1983). Relationships between office characteristics and employee reactions: A study of the physical environment. *Administrative Science Quarterly*, *28*, 542–556.

Wall, T. D., Jackson, P. R., Mullarkey, S., & Parker, S. K. (1996).

The demands-control model of job strain: A more specific test. *Journal of Occupational and Organizational Psychology*, *69*, 153–166.

Warr, P. B. (1990). Decision latitude, job demands and employee well-being. *Work and Stress*, *4*, 285–294.

Wrzesniewski, A., & Dutton, J. E. (2001). Crafting a job: Revisioning employees as active crafters of their work. *Academy of Management Review*, *26*, 179–201.

Xie, J. L., & Johns, G. (1995). Job scope and stress: Can job scope be too high? *Academy of Management Journal*, *38*, 1288–1309.

Chapter 6: What's in a job? 2. When enough is enough

Colquitt, J. A., Conlon, D. E., Wesson, M. J., Porter, C. O. L. H., & Ng, K. Y. (2001). Justice at the millennium: A meta-analytic review of 25 years of organizational justice research. *Journal of Applied Psychology*, *86*, 425–445.

Judge, T. A., Piccolo, R. F., & Ilies, R. (2004). The forgotten ones? The validity of consideration and initiating structure in leadership research. *Journal of Applied Psychology*, *89*, 36–51.

Sverke, M., Hellgren, J., & Näswall, K. (2002). No security: A meta-analysis and review of job insecurity and its consequences. *Journal of Occupational Health Psychology*, *7*, 242–264.

Taris, T. W., Kalimo, R., & Schaufeli, W. B. (2002). Inequity at work: Its measurement and association with worker health. *Work and Stress*, *16*, 287–301.

Tepper, B. J. (2000). Consequences of abusive supervision. *Academy of Management Journal*, *43*, 178–190.

Chapter 7: It's in your genes as well as your job

Arvey, R. D., McCall, B. P., Bouchard, T. J., Taubman, P., & Cavanaugh, M. A. (1994). Genetic influences on job satisfaction and work values. *Personality and Individual Differences*, *17*, 21–33.

DeNeve, K. M., & Cooper, H. (1998). The happy personality: A meta-analysis of 137 personality traits and subjective well-being. *Psychological Bulletin*, *124*, 197–229.

Diener, E., & Lucas, R. E. (1999). Personality and subjective well-being. In D. Kahneman, E. Diener, and N. Schwartz (eds.), *Well-being: The foundations of hedonic psychology* (pp. 213–229). New York: Russell Sage Foundation.

Headey, B., & Wearing, A. (1989). Personality, life events, and subjective well-being: Toward a dynamic equilibrium model. *Journal of Personality and Social Psychology, 57,* 731–739.

Judge, T. A., Heller, D., & Mount, M. K. (2002). Five-factor model of personality and job satisfaction: A meta-analysis. *Journal of Applied Psychology, 87,* 530–541.

Staw, B. M., & Cohen-Charash, Y. (2005). The dispositional approach to job satisfaction: More than a mirage, but not yet an oasis. *Journal of Organizational Behavior, 26,* 59–78.

Chapter 8: Come to think about it . . . happiness is relative

Boswell, W. R., Boudreau, J. W., & Tichy, J. (2005). The relationship between employee job change and job satisfaction: The honeymoon-hangover effect. *Journal of Applied Psychology, 90,* 882–892.

Clark, A. E., & Oswald, A. J. (1996). Satisfaction and comparison income. *Journal of Public Economics, 61,* 359–381.

Roese, N. J., & Olson, J. M. (1995) (eds.). *What might have been: The social psychology of counterfactual thinking.* Mahwah, NJ: Erlbaum.

Sheldon, K. M., & Houser-Marko, L. (2001). Self-concordance, goal attainment, and the pursuit of happiness: Can there be an upward spiral? *Journal of Personality and Social Psychology, 80,* 152–165.

Suls, J., & Wheeler, L. (2000) (eds.), *Handbook of social comparison: Theory and research.* New York: Kluwer/Plenum.

Wanous, J. P., Poland, T. D., Premack, S. L., & Davis, K. S. (1992). The effects of met expectations on newcomer attitudes and behaviors: A review and meta-analysis. *Journal of Applied Psychology, 77,* 288–297.

Warr, P. B. (2006). Differential activation of judgments in employee well-being. *Journal of Occupational and Organizational Psychology, 79,* 225–244.

Warr, P. B. (2008). Work values: Some demographic and cultural correlates. *Journal of Occupational and Organizational Psychology, 81,* 751–775.

Index